TELOS MOVIE CLASSICS

HULK

TELOS MOVIE CLASSICS

HULK

TONY LEE

First published in the UK in 2012 by

Telos Publishing Ltd

17 Pendre Avenue, Prestatyn, Denbighshire LL19 9SH

www.telos.co.uk

Telos Publishing Ltd values feedback. Please e-mail us with any comments
you may have about this book to: feedback@telos.co.uk

ISBN: 978-1-84583-066-3

Telos Movie Classics: Hulk © 2012 Tony Lee

The moral right of the author has been asserted.

Internal design, typesetting and layout by Arnold T Blumberg
www.atbpublishing.com

Printed in the UK by Berforts Group Ltd

British Library Cataloguing in Publication Data.

A catalogue record for this book is available from the British Library.

'And thine omnipotence a crown of pain,
To cling like burning gold round thy dissolving brain'

Prometheus Unbound (1820)

Percy Bysshe Shelley

ANGER MANAGEMENT: INTRODUCTION

I first saw Ang Lee's movie *Hulk* on 23 July 2003, at my local multiplex. Before that visit to the cinema, I had already seen the one-minute teaser-trailer, which draws us into a domestic vignette. The voiceover expresses fretful thoughts about losing control, and confesses, ominously: 'I like it.'

I liked it, too. The teaser is an ingeniously composed sketch about irresistible and uncontrollable power unleashed, accomplishing a lot with its moment of chilling anxiety that gives way to a dramatic outburst of extraordinarily violent intensity. It hints at the movie's intelligent dramas, and its keenly psychological approach to pulp material, suggesting that it will be a wholly fascinating science fictional treatment of super-heroism that is a big screen equivalent to the highly sophisticated genre mode of Warren Ellis's or Alan Moore's finest comicbook works.

Another one minute long *Hulk* trailer, shown on American TV in a high-profile slot during coverage of the 2003 NFL Super Bowl match on 26 January 2003, is an expressionist affair of compacted footage, specifically highlighting both widescreen action and intimate drama scenes from the then-unfinished movie. Like the teaser, it leads with a narration: 'I don't know who I am. I don't know what I'm … becoming.' It sets up the narrative centrepiece of deeply troubled relationships, and it displays aspects of the Hulk's phenomenal abilities, as revealed by vivid snapshots, to establish the magnificent scale of this

Hollywood project by Universal Studios.

With a tongue-in-cheek effect, the mild-mannered voiceover assures viewers of one thing: 'You wouldn't like me when I'm angry' – an instantly recognisable line from the popular late-1970s/early-1980s TV show *The Incredible Hulk*. However, it's a conventionally constructed advert compared with the intriguing teaser. Its main value is to make it clear to the many fans of Marvel comics that Ang Lee's characterisation of the Hulk would match the original comicbook Hulk's super-powers of prodigious strength with a giant size. Happily, this movie was not going to be a simplified or scaled-down version of the Hulk, as previously seen in the TV show. The first authentic adaptation of its comicbook source material, *Hulk* shows its protagonist creature going on a full-blown rampage, capable of destroying anything that gets in his way.

As I began watching the movie in the cinema for the first time, it struck me as quite amusing that *Hulk* presents us with a couple of odd coincidences. The main character of Bruce Banner is played by Australian actor Eric Bana. In addition to the curiosity of those sound-alike names, the Hulk was originally created by American comicbook writer Stan Lee, while *Hulk* is directed by Taiwanese filmmaker Ang Lee (obviously, no relation). Writing this book adds my name to the string of coincidence, and I'm not related to either of them.

My first impression of Ang Lee's *Hulk* was that I had just seen the greatest comicbook adaptation ever made. Not only did the movie fulfil all of my expectations as a fan of Marvel comics, it greatly surpassed them. It was, in its complexity and sophistication, a far superior entertainment (for a summer blockbuster, at least!) than I had thought mainstream Hollywood was still capable of producing. I felt that this was also the very best genre movie I had seen for well over a decade. *Hulk* set a new, and astonishingly high, standard for inspired artistry in the subgenre of superhero cinema. It crafted a solemnly ambiguous and deeply resonant modern myth from an essentially pulpy source. *Hulk* achieved a paradigm shift in the sci-fi and fantasy subgenre of comicbook adaptations that would not be matched closely until the release of Christopher Nolan's excellent crime thriller *The Dark Knight* (2008). Ang Lee's movie is marvellously successful as an exciting SF adventure, as a scary monster movie, as a doomed fairytale romance, as a conspiracy thriller, as a technological horror story, as a profoundly human tragedy, as an uncompromisingly literate and subtle adaptation of a comicbook and television icon, and as a groundbreaking visual effects masterpiece. *Hulk* is all of these things, and more.

There is a qualitative difference between making a comicbook style movie, and making a movie that is based upon superhero comics. It all depends on the process of adaptation from page to screen, and whether the filmmakers are slavishly faithful to the comicbook source, or choose to deviate radically from what's been widely accepted as canonical material. Changes to plots are made in order to fulfil the demands of contemporary cinematic artistry over traditional comicbook tropes. This tricky process of adaptation is not about diluting the purity of a comicbook format, but concerned with selecting all of the original's best ideas and then adding extra relevant dimensions. Of course, there can be no objective critical analysis of this creative matter, especially when we must take into consideration whether or not the viewer has previously read the original comics and, in the case of Ang Lee's *Hulk*, also seen *The Incredible Hulk* TV series. Any reportage or reviewing based upon unemotional observations is either impossible or largely flawed. Two or more people can actually like, or dislike, the very same thing, but often for different reasons.

Despite its wonderfully evocative opening montage, Zack Snyder's *Watchmen* (2009) is simply too devoted to realising Alan Moore's 1980s graphic novel upon the big screen to be fully effective as a piece of 21st Century cinema. *Watchmen* has several excellent sequences detailing the conflicts of uncompromising moral forces against the imperfections of human nature, albeit presented as mere superhero punch-ups, but its retro futurism and alternative history plotline serve up a mishmash of fleeting sci-fi horrors and somewhat dull soap opera, even in the director's cut version. Elsewhere in the grand multiverse of comicbook adventures, Guillermo del Toro's *Hellboy* (2004) very wisely added something new and vital to the existing milieu created by writer and artist Mike Mignola. In the superb movie, paranormal investigator Hellboy (Ron Perlman) has an on/off romantic partnership with BPRD agent Liz Sherman (Selma Blair). While she has pyrokinetic powers, Hellboy is fireproof. They are quite simply made for each other. This combo works so well, and so in favour of the weird and occult scenario, that *Hellboy* remains writer-director del Toro's best work to date.

In my January 2004 review of Universal's DVD release of Ang Lee's *Hulk* (for VideoVista monthly webzine at www. videovista.net), I concluded: '*Hulk* is the most supremely imaginative genre adventure since *RoboCop*.' Although the overall tone of Lee's undervalued magnum opus is markedly different from that of the edgy media satire and briskly paced splattery violence that distinguished Paul Verhoeven's 1987 US debut, *Hulk* shares with *RoboCop* a package of refreshing qualities, not the least of which is a foreigner's view of American politicking, corporate cultural trends, dysfunctional families, and other social problems.

Was it nature or nurture that made the Hulk such a formidable character? What are the cultural and aesthetic influences and the literary inspirations that informed both Stan Lee and Jack Kirby's *The Incredible Hulk*, and Ang Lee's *Hulk*? Who are David and Bruce Banner? How could memories of a 25-year-old television series affect the box-office appeal and critical reception of a 21st Century movie? Why did we have to wait so long for a realistic version of the comicbook Hulk to appear on screen?

Hulk is – for me, at least – the first genuinely classic movie of the 21st Century. This book will examine the richness of the movie's narrative content, in which the dualistic protagonist lurches toward an Aristotelian catastrophe, and consider the highly impressive diversity of genre themes explored in *Hulk*, while I attempt to answer those and other questions.

For this comprehensive study, I have included some background information and selected a few plot details – where particularly relevant to the movie – from the official novelisation, *Hulk* by Peter David, 'based on the motion picture screenplay written by James Schamus' (published by Boxtree, 2003).

CHAPTER ONE: ANXIETY & THE BOMB: INFLUENCES

'If you've ever had any experience with a two-year-old who has not gotten what he or she wants at the supermarket, you've had an experience with the Hulk.'

– James Schamus, interviewed in
Hulk: The Official Souvenir Movie Magazine
(Titan Publishing, summer 2003)

When I was a boy and I outgrew reading such famous British weeklies as the *Dandy* and the *Beano*, I became a fan of Marvel comics. With all their strange, amazing, incredible, uncanny, and frequently bizarre characters, Marvel offered a vast universe of escapism to explore that was (unlike the majority of DC comics) largely focused upon locations in the real world – albeit usually American cities like New York. Even though their adventure stories usually described a colourful diversity that lacked proper narrative coherence, I found superheroes to be inspiring figures: they were the new space-age equivalents of the champions of legend (such as King Arthur) and folklore (like Robin Hood), or the fantastic pantheons of ancient Greek and Roman mythologies. In several cases, Marvel's characters actually *were* timeless versions of those same immortals and demigods (Hercules, for example) from the familiar myths. Superhero comicbooks are the best combination of SF and fantasy to be found in any entertainment medium. The mixing of different genres rarely works as well in cinema or television.

The comicbook Hulk was not so much a fusion of those oft-cited 19th Century literary classics Mary Shelley's *Frankenstein* and Robert Louis Stevenson's *Strange Case of Dr Jekyll and Mr Hyde* as it was inspired by the filmed versions of them. In particular, basic genre concepts for the Hulk can be found in James Whale's *Frankenstein* (1931) – which starred Boris Karloff – and one or more of the screen versions of the 'Jekyll and Hyde' story made in 1931 (Paramount) and 1941 (MGM), or perhaps in Terence Fisher's *The Two Faces of Dr Jekyll* (1960) – shot in vivid Technicolor by Hammer Studios. The traditional fairytale *Beauty and the Beast* and the RKO movie *King Kong* (1933) are the other main thematic ancestors of the Hulk.

From Karloff's classic portrayal of Frankenstein's monster, the Hulk of the comicbooks draws his slow-wittedness and his behaviour as a lumbering creature. The influence of Jekyll and Hyde is readily apparent in the way, if not the means, by which the usually quite civilised scientist Dr Banner undergoes induced transformations to expose his repressed and usually savage alter-ego, the Hulk. In the brutish Hulk's encounters with monster-tamer Betty Ross, we find a sci-fi reflection of *Beauty and the Beast*, while in his animalistic rampages there is a clear reference to *King Kong*. The genius of Ang Lee's direction of *Hulk* lies, partly, in returning to those very same genre influences as the primary sources of literary inspiration for his movie, while exploring fresher 21st Century perspectives of them, rather than simply taking cues from the original comicbook story's previous, variably effective, interpretations.

13

In *Hulk*, while Bruce is held by Ross's military at the underground Desert Base, he's allowed outside for a stroll with Betty through the ruined town above the complex. The couple reminisce about their childhoods, and realise that they both lived in the same place when they were kids. Bruce finds his family's old house. Confronting the ghosts of his past, he stands nervously before the closed door that haunts his dreams, but the room, of course, is empty now. It's a scene Ang Lee chose to shoot quickly, using available light and a handheld camera, giving Bruce's emotionally raw homecoming a realistic and yet disquietingly eerie mood.

It is a clever play upon the archetypal romantic themes of *Beauty and the Beast*, as the abandoned residence of Bruce's childhood stands in marked contrast to the Beast's palatial castle home. Unlike the virginal Belle with her cursed prince in the fairytale, Betty is a realist who is trying to understand the monster within the man, not release the man trapped behind the visage of the Beast. Betty's effort to discover psychological links between the Hulk and Bruce is, in many ways, a farewell sequence. Eschewing the handy props of that old fairytale, there is no enchanted mirror to view beyond human perception, no magic ring in Betty's world, and she will not live happily ever after with Bruce. They are both grown ups now.

High above San Francisco, during the Hulk's long fall after his final encounter with the jets, there is a surreal flashback to Bruce's shaving scene (which was the adult character's introduction in *Hulk*, but here is a memory heightened by imagination). When Bruce wipes condensation off the oversized mirror, the Hulk glares back at him from the other side of the glass, with a giant finger matching the arcing movement of Bruce's palm. Smashing through the imaginary looking-glass, to conflate dream and explication, the Hulk grabs Bruce and intones the monster's popular catchphrase (from the comicbook series): 'Puny human.'

It is the first time that the Hulk *speaks* in this movie but, of course, he is not actually *talking*, because the schizoid confrontation occurs only in the subconscious mind of the dual character. Whether or not the Hulk is aware that he actually is Bruce, it's made perfectly clear what the monster thinks of the man. The novelisation is especially perceptive about this odd psychological mirroring scene: 'They regard each other like two old friends and two old enemies, all interconnected' (page 309, *Hulk* by Peter David, Boxtree, 2003). In its purposeful reflection of Jekyll and Hyde themes, this echoes Matthew Modine's character Private 'Joker' Davis in Stanley Kubrick's scathing antiwar drama *Full Metal Jacket* (1987): 'I was trying to suggest something about the duality of man ... the Jungian thing.' Amongst other things, the Hulk is very much the embodiment of both a symbol of peace and a creature that's born to kill.

When Ross pursues the Hulk onto Telegraph Hill in San Francisco, there is a ceasefire, although the 'Angry Man' is surrounded by cops and troops, with jets and helicopters circling above the scene. Ross lands his command Huey so that

Betty can confront the beast. She approaches him, their eyes meet, and the Hulk begins shrinking, while oozing fluids into a spreading puddle (no erectile dysfunction jokes, please!), as the severely weakened Bruce almost collapses. Betty kneels down to hug Bruce and she cries for him, while the security forces edge closer to the reunited couple. Even army hard-man Ross looks almost tearful as he's watching them on the street.

It's the only time in this movie that we see the Hulk change back into Bruce in broad daylight, and Ang Lee opts to show this in a dazzling combination of live-action and flawless CG animation, without any close-up inserts like those used to show transformations in *The Incredible Hulk* TV series. It is a dazzling sequence of visual effects that demonstrates, in a unique fashion, why it has taken several decades for this movie finally to be produced. Until very recently, the film-making technology required for any wholly realistic portrayal of the comicbook Hulk's character simply did not exist.

Betty and the beast serves as a fairytale closure to *Hulk*'s main sci-fi monster-movie rampage. Although Betty has saved Bruce from his green-skinned alter-ego, she realises that there is no future for him and they can never be together. Betty believes that she has probably – if not inevitably – doomed Bruce to a life of solitary confinement. As the Hulk, at least, he could have been free.

We have seen this kind of deeply romanticised twist ending to an existential crisis before. Just as the Hulk appears to have made Bruce a slave to his own rage, so Eddie Jessup's vaulting ambition and incurable curiosity seem to have doomed his physical human existence in the first climactic sequence of Ken Russell's *Altered States* (1980). Almost consumed by the whirlpool of an apparently cosmic energy, unleashed by his experiments in sensory deprivation, Eddie (William Hurt, in a breakthrough performance) surrenders to the self-destructive phenomena of a transcendental dead end. What saves Eddie's psyche in the electrifying finale of *Altered States* is the proverbial power of love. When Eddie's ex-wife Emily (Blair Brown) intervenes, she risks her own sanity to reach down into the swirling fogs and drag Eddie back from the brink. *Hulk* subtly mirrors that intervention, as Betty draws Bruce back to a semblance of emotional stability, returning him to a reality of human scale.

Weird Science

When the original comicbook's Dr Banner first transforms into the Hulk, and establishes the man-monster's nature as initially aggressive – the Hulk's first words are: 'Get out of my way, insect!' (*The Incredible Hulk* #1, page five) – the scene cribs from Jekyll and Hyde. Instead of that genre borrowing, Ang Lee's movie version draws upon the even greater strangeness of Frankenstein's monster, as the innocent Hulk appears in Bruce's lab, and the creature meets his metaphorical creator/ biological father, David, on the way out. David's encounters with the monster in *Hulk* have other shades of meaning, too (as explained in the following chapters).

This follows in the oversized footsteps of the TV show's homage to James Whale's classic *Frankenstein*, as the pilot

17

episode of *The Incredible Hulk* includes a scene where the creature spots a little girl fishing beside a lake and, when the scared girl wades thoughtlessly into the water until she's out of her depth, the Hulk uproots a tree, to use like a lifeguard's reach pole, in a well-intentioned effort to save the frightened child from drowning. However, as in the aforementioned *Frankenstein* movie, the Hulk's rescue attempt is misunderstood: the girl's outdoorsman father returns from hunting nearby and unthinkingly shoots and wounds the Hulk.

In the TV pilot, Banner's partner in his genetic research, Dr Elaina Marks (Susan Sullivan), is the first and probably the only person he can turn to for help. 'I remember being incredibly strong,' he says to her, while he's trying to overcome his loss of memory after his first change into the Hulk. Unlike Betty in the comicbook story, Elaina is a scientist, and her character is an obvious influence upon how Betty is written for Ang Lee's *Hulk*. As expected, there is a sense of unrequited love between the lead characters, Banner and Elaina, in the first *The Incredible Hulk* TV movie, but any reciprocal demonstration of affection is interrupted and sidelined by further developments of the main plot.

Working with Elaina, Banner agrees to be locked inside the secluded laboratory's hyperbaric pressure chamber, using it as a containment space for the controlled experiment, designed to trigger another metamorphosis. There is a chilling noir style to the shadowy lighting of the TV movie's set designs for these scenes, adding the gothic atmosphere of classic sci-fi horror movies (like *Frankenstein*) to this contemporary hi-tech scenario. This identifies *The Incredible Hulk* TV series as an intermediate form of the character's developing mythology, one still clinging to styles of the past. In *Hulk*, Ang Lee eschews much of that gothic atmosphere in favour of a hi-tech realism that's more appealing to audiences in the 21st Century.

Although initial tests fail, Banner endures a nightmare, causing him sufficient agitation to change again, as his dream about the Hulk becomes a reality. Feeling imprisoned, the Hulk breaks out through the lab vault's chromium steel airlock, and this particular TV movie sequence is cleverly re-enacted for *Hulk*, but in somewhat different circumstances, and with greater poignancy, becoming a more primal scene about rebirth.

In the TV movie, nervous but fascinated scientist Elaina provides an intelligently observant (no blonde moments for her!) and suspenseful commentary: 'Intelligence level drops; and primitive emotions take over the brain and the body.' After the raging creature escapes from the sealed chamber, Banner and Elaina both realise, at last, that the Hulk is not a safe subject for any close study, yet Banner persists in considering other possibilities for finding a cure: 'I wanna be Dr Banner, not Dr Jekyll.' Although Jekyll is not mentioned in *Hulk*, the movie's screenplay astutely references the genre themes of Jekyll and Hyde on several occasions.

The young David (Bruce's father) in *Hulk* conducts experiments to isolate factors of green bioluminescence, regeneration, tissue hardening and resistance to toxins, as rapid defence mechanisms that protect life against pain or injuries. He achieves a 'stable combination' of mixed and matched DNA, ready for live animal testing but, like Dr Jekyll, he is not satisfied with the mediocrity of the time-honoured scientific method, and his ambition drives him to perform the test upon himself, whatever the consequences. Obviously, David is not the epitome of scientific virtue, and his actions serve as a postmodern reflection upon other traditional science fiction icons (see Chapter Two). In contrast to *Hulk*'s tacit incorporation of Jekyll and Hyde into its broad range of genre tropes, Stephen Norrington's movie, *The League of Extraordinary Gentlemen* (2003) – also derived from a comicbook – featured a version of Mr Hyde who is something of a *hulky* beast-man, but a much less effective CGI character than the green giant of *Hulk*.

On the Rampage

During the comicbook Hulk's first transformation, the escaping monster wrecks an army jeep, and one of the men who survives the crash reports: 'I wouldn't be surprised if he was a giant gorilla that escaped from some zoo!' (*The Incredible Hulk* #1, page 13). The soldier's testimony is illustrated with the sketchy image of an ape that alludes to *King Kong*. Dr Banner is clearly traumatised by his first transformation into the Hulk, but he suspects the worst is yet to come, and fears that, when night falls, he will change once again, 'into that brutal, bestial mockery of a human – that creature which fears nothing – which despises reason and worships power!' (*The*

Incredible Hulk #1, page 14), and he's not wrong to worry. The loss of reason, in favour of instinct, is a major theme in nearly every version of the Hulk's mythology.

Apart from revising the *Beauty and the Beast* moments that most versions of *King Kong* have explored previously, the most deliberate riffs upon *King Kong* in *Hulk* are the breakout from captivity in the Desert Base sequence, and the subsequent action of Hulk versus the Comanche stealth gunships – which pays tribute to John Guillermin's 1976 remake of *King Kong*, in which the great ape is attacked by a trio of US Army helicopters. As in that underrated movie, where the great ape is harassed by airborne weapons of man's technology, *Hulk* sees the green giant buried alive and, obviously, left for dead by the attacking rotorcraft. In the three foremost versions of *King Kong*, the ape falls to its death at the end. *Hulk* features two scenes where the creature *survives* falling. First, while battling the dogs, the Hulk is toppled from his treetop perch in the forest. Secondly, in his ride on the back of a warplane, he is carried up to the edge of space. In the original *King Kong* of 1933, the ape climbs to the top of the Empire State building, and is attacked by bi-planes. *Hulk* pays tribute to that by showing jets attacking the Hulk's vantage point on the Golden Gate Bridge, and follows that with the Hulk's long drop into San Francisco bay from the plane's climb into the sky. It is an amusing variation on common themes of ascension and inevitable descent – as what goes up must come down, for an effective allegory of the Greek myth of Icarus's escape from Crete (though without a conclusion that involves drowning, obviously!)

Ron Koslow's TV series *Beauty and the Beast* (1987-1990) was a romantic fantasy showcasing urban action sequences that were very much like superhero adventures. Fifteen years before he starred in *Hellboy*, Ron Perlman played lion-man Vincent in this show. He lives in an underground hideaway for outcasts, from where he becomes the beloved protector of a New York assistant district attorney, Catherine (Linda Hamilton). Much like the superhero TV series *Lois & Clark: the New Adventures of Superman* (1993-1997), which soon followed it, *Beauty and the Beast* was a fairytale in revisionist mode, but still adhered to a classic theme, with its noble hero who frequently rescues a damsel in distress. *Hulk* draws inspiration from that vigilante interpretation of the fairytale, and takes it one step further in the sequence where the Hulk saves Betty from the mutant dogs, and in the reunion where Betty (metaphorically) *rescues* Bruce from the Hulk in San Francisco. This complex interweaving of tragic love story with scenes of antihero action is an updated *Beauty and the Beast* that adds further layers of genre resonance to *Hulk*.

Of all the postwar science fiction movies, Fred M Wilcox's *Forbidden Planet* (1956) stands out from other pulpy offerings as the finest genre classic of that era. It was inspired by William Shakespeare's play *The Tempest* (circa 1610), and its space opera framing plot explores an inexplicable release of the antagonistic Monster from the Id, in a scenario where intellect is overwhelmed by a primal force of nature. A projection from the subconscious mind of scientist Dr Morbius (Walter Pidgeon), the rampaging yet invisible being is generated by the atomic technology of a failed and extinct alien race. Human defences are unable to stop the Id monster for long, and it is only when Morbius accepts the truth about the mysterious energy-being's existence that the protagonists are safe from harm.

From the moment that David transforms into his superhuman form, Ang Lee's *Hulk* shifts gears into wholly surrealistic imagery that pays affectionate tribute to *Forbidden Planet*'s bizarre, seemingly unstoppable engine of conflict. The grand finale of *Hulk* is a spectacular piece of visual imagination and comes as close to depicting a battle of the gods as any work of cinema has ever achieved.

Colossal Dangers

Aside from the classic literary influences and their attendant adaptations for the cinema screen, a more direct genre predecessor to Stan Lee and Jack Kirby's synthetic mythology of the Hulk was Bert I Gordon's B-movie *The Amazing Colossal Man* (1957) and its sequel *War of the Colossal Beast* (1968), which can perhaps be regarded as the human-monster movie response to atomic-era creature features like *Godzilla* (1954) and *Them!* (1954). Viewable as the cult fandom counterpart to Jack Arnold's SF classic *The Incredible Shrinking Man* – also dated 1957 but released seven months earlier – schlock favourite *The Amazing Colossal Man* (from American International Pictures), sees Colonel Glenn Manning (Glenn Langan) trying to save a downed pilot from certain death, only to be caught out in the open and exposed to the nuclear blast of a plutonium bomb test. Radiation trauma results in a limited chance of survival for Manning, who managed to shield his eyes with his arms, but 'who hasn't a square inch of skin left on his entire body.' While swathed in bandages, Manning unexpectedly grows a whole new skin, overnight. This miraculous process has replaced dead tissue without leaving any scars, but now Manning is bald.

Army scientists consider his case worth studying for the potential of tapping into a remarkable healing power, but Manning's cell regeneration appears to be unstoppable and, when he regains consciousness, he grows into a 30-foot giant weighing over 2,000 pounds. Allowed to see Manning, because she has a calming influence on his troubled psyche, Manning's fiancée Carol (Cathy Downs) fulfils a role similar to that of heroine Ann Darrow (Fay Wray) in *King Kong*. Manning admits that he feels the disturbing estrangement of living in a shrinking world, and worries that he is slowly turning crazy from being a circus freak, while he's wearing an adjustable sarong like a baby's nappy (well, at least the Hulk keeps his trousers!).

However, the increasingly restless Manning escapes from captivity, kidnaps Carol, and eventually goes on the rampage, causing a panic on the streets of Las Vegas. Eventually, the 60-foot Manning is cornered by troops at the Hoover Dam, where he releases Carol, but the giant man is promptly shot and falls into the Colorado River, in a briskly-paced finale essentially copied from *King Kong* – also rather unsubtly evoked by this B-movie's poster artwork.

Producer and director Gordon, who is also credited with special technical effects work, co-wrote *The Amazing Colossal Man* with Mark Hanna, who went on to do the screenplay for *Attack of the 50 Foot Woman* (1958). Gordon's cheap and cheerful effort recycles stock footage of US nuclear tests and suffers from the typical 1950s sci-fi syndrome of having terrible visual effects. These include the supposedly gigantic Manning on miniature sets or superimposed against landmarks on a back-projection screen, with double exposures, often created without mattes, for shoddy process work that makes him appear semi-transparent. Technical faults aside, *The Amazing Colossal Man* benefits from its rudimentary science fictional explanations, which are adequate for such genre movies of the era, while its fairly preposterous scenario, about a victim of an A-bomb test growing to 'about ten times the size of a normal man,' provides a template for similar mutational effects explored in *The Incredible Hulk* comicbook.

Another subgenre precursor to the Hulk is Allan Dwan's low-budget cult flick *Most Dangerous Man Alive* (1961). This concerns gangster Eddie Candell (Ron Randell), who escapes from police custody and flees across a nuclear testing site where he's affected by a new element, 'cobalt isotope X', from A-bomb radiation. The exposure causes his body to absorb metals, and his flesh mutates into living steel, making him bullet-proof, and Eddie uses his newfound invulnerability for vengeance. Although the super-power acquired by Eddie makes him seem rather more like the mutant *X-Men* character Colossus (created by Len Wein and Dave Cockrum for Marvel in 1975) than the Hulk, the atomic weapon source of his immense strength, his slow decline into a terminally violent rage, and the redemptive drama that unfolds between him and his sympathetic girlfriend Carla Angelo (Elaine Stewart) ensure this rarely-seen movie deserves a place in the line-up of genre forerunners to *The Incredible Hulk* comicbook.

If they are considered as a pair, the movies are more than a doodle of origin concepts, and practically a rough sketch of the Hulk character all ready for Stan Lee and Jack Kirby to add further layers to. Genre references to *King Kong* and *Beauty and the Beast* are identifiable in *The Amazing Colossal Man*, so all the comicbook creators needed to do was infuse the story with *Frankenstein* science and filter the psychological transformation through Jekyll and Hyde. The resulting formula combines everything with a surprisingly impressive neatness.

Directorial Vision

'My Hulk has to be more than an embodiment of human strength.'

> – Ang Lee, interviewed in
> *Hulk: The Official Souvenir Movie Magazine*
> (Titan Publishing, summer 2003)

Ang Lee's filmmaking career started with intimate and melancholic family dramas like *The Ice Storm* (1997) before he made the art-house Western *Ride with the Devil* (1999) and the masterly chanbara *Crouching Tiger, Hidden Dragon*

(2000), featuring a legendary weapon called Green Destiny. The martial arts drama became the winner of multiple awards (including a set of Oscars, BAFTAs and Golden Globes) and the most successful foreign-language movie in American box-office history. The themes of bewilderment and introspection that distinguished Lee's earlier character-driven pictures are also found in *Hulk*, and yet here they are connected to, and contrasted with, an almost boundless exhilaration of deeply imaginative freedom, as *Hulk* represents both poles of intensive philosophical thought. In addition to infusing the emotive aspects of Greek tragedies into the psychologically complex storyline, the director explores state-of-the-art technical innovations within a unique comicbook aestheticism in this movie's often astonishing visuals.

Unlike the simplicity of the original comicbook's gamma bomb explosion, or the TV show's use of just a radiation device for creating the Hulk, this first cinema adaptation includes the satisfying complexity of dark psychodrama in its origin story. This treatment neatly reflects upon the evolution of the Hulk character over 40 years' worth of comicbook adventures, and at the same time explores the speculative possibilities of an updated origin for the Hulk that is informed by the 21st Century's promise of great scientific advances to come from a mix of genetic engineering and nanotechnology.

Hulk is supremely effective as the key to early 21st Century genre movie projects because of the painstaking effort contributed by Ang Lee, dealing with great actors, while also pushing for the finest CGI creativity to date from the

ILM company's various artists and technicians. The movie is acceptable as action spectacular in a realistic mode partly because of the televised scenes of massive urban destruction in New York on 11 September 2001. Demolition of the World Trade Centre skyscrapers by jihad terrorists with hijacked aeroplanes shocked the world. Even more so when it emerged that such a farfetched militant Islamic plot was linked to al-Qaeda founder Osama bin Laden – perhaps the world's first actual super-villain. After what is commonly called 9/11, the perceptual and conceptual gulf between normality and the weirdness of a comicbook movie universe had narrowed considerably. It is easy enough to imagine airliners crashing into a skyscraper for a disaster movie but, until soon after the millennium, it was practically unthinkable that it could happen in reality. Furthermore, the epic showdown in *Hulk* between the rampaging creature and Ross's military forces demonstrates the fallacy of the so-called *war on terror*, because terrorism simply cannot be defeated by the small-minded and nihilistic approach of trying to fight fire with fire.

Ang Lee also explores a consistent fascination with nature in *Hulk*. Although digital maps and military tracking displays chart the Hulk's rapid progress when he is pursued by Ross's army forces, it is the shaded oasis of trees, shrubs and assorted greenery where the Hulk takes a breather on his transcontinental journey that fully captures the director's awed attention. The Hulk sits down and stares in mute wonder at various types of plants, as if he is rather surprised to find anything at all living in the largely barren region.

28

It is only one of many elegiac scenes in *Hulk* where the unspoilt beauty of the natural world is disturbed by mankind's mechanised acts of violence. This aspect of the movie seems to be channelling the environmental concerns of John Boorman's *The Emerald Forest* (1985), a spectacularly *green* drama, based upon a true story in which an American engineer (Powers Boothe) searches for his missing son (Charley Boorman) in the Brazilian rainforest. In the poetic coda of *Hulk*, we see the fugitive Bruce as a medical aid worker far south of the border, paying a tactful homage to the consciousness-raising impact of Boorman's ecological fable.

Hulk confirms Ang Lee as a master of emotional intensity and cinematic lyricism, as this movie is a seamless fusion of pop culture and serious drama. The director's earnest commitment to challenging fandom perspectives of the Hulk's comicbook character is matched by the movie's unconventional editing style, which develops compositions and transitions, from shot to shot and scene to scene, with an organic momentum that we have not seen before or since in a Hollywood blockbuster production. The aesthetics of moving split-screens and CGI transitions have the cumulative affect of an entirely visual *narrator*; a stand-in for the written narration of comicbooks. *Hulk* still follows the golden rule of cinematic exposition by showing instead of telling and, in doing so, its experimental creativity and innovation add to the vocabulary of film language.

As revealed in the DVD and Blu-ray disc bonus features and behind-the-scenes extras about making the movie, Ang

Lee himself performed some of the motion capture work (in a 'mo-cap' suit, with markers to record digital information about his body's movements), which informs the unique Hulk character with a chaotic sensibility. This provided a shortcut to blueprint data for ILM animators, so the Hulk appears more lifelike on-screen, and it's a pervasive simulation of a radical persona.

Frameworks

The introductory scenes of *Hulk* establish the overall tone for the movie's artistic stylisation of science fiction imagery. Danny Elfman's theme music leads into a colourful animation that links the formation of cosmic matter in the Big Bang to cellular blobs that display evolutionary theory on super-fast-forward. In the first of many signature framing shots, a bank of video monitors resembles the panels of a comicbook page. There are reverse jump-cuts and split-screens, and one computer-graphic display hovers in mid-air like a comicbook thought-bubble. Background elements cut into the foreground. It's a very info-rich environment, designed so that our views of interior sets or landscapes are constantly switching angles as the highly creative framing and fluid editing of varied shots generate a keen sense of suspense and energy without the need for very much technical dialogue.

There are multiple images and arrays of data screens, which are sometimes shuffled around like a conjuror using a pack of cards. Virtual 3D holographic layouts have cropped frames shifting, overlapping and continuously re-sizing, but without losing sight of the main focus in any particular scene. Innovative transitional effects use CGI for the editing process. Scenes are cut and pasted together in a dynamic and eclectic but immersive fashion, with slow wipes or quick swipes and punchy close-ups, deployed or positioned in a highly distinctive and often provocative approach to screen narrative continuity that is rarely less than mesmerising to watch. TV action series *24* (2001-2010) also used many split-screen visuals for storytelling, but *Hulk* takes this to an entirely new level of invention.

Digital editing techniques enable rapid montages borrowing the snapshots approach of sequential art in modern comicbooks, depicting a surrealistic backdrop, which can be used to pin up memories as flashback illustrations of Bruce's fluctuating state of mind, and to show glimpses of his inner turmoil – as if capturing displays of his every fleeting thought. The use of comicbook style panels as a cascade of framing devices in *Hulk* shows us, more vividly than ever before or since, the mental processes involved in the imaginative reading of superhero comics. These sequences in *Hulk* display what may be occurring in the mind's eye of the comicbook reader, linking together static artwork by filling in all the gaps to create a surrealist narrative motion in the reader's headspace; and, as such, *Hulk* accomplishes – for the first time in the history of comicbook adaptations – a precise visual allegory of comicbook imagery at work in the imagination, showing how readers perceive the sequential art in words and pictures.

To see and better understand how this works, consider the

31

so-often-misunderstood auteurism of Michael Bay's trilogy of *Transformers* movies (2007-2011). In the wake of *Hulk*, these sci-fi adventures, based upon a range of toys made by the Hasbro Company, perfectly depict what's going on in a child's mind while playing with these now collectible shape-changing robots. Although, perhaps, drawing visual cues from watching the cartoon series produced in the mid-1980s, children allow their imaginations to run riot while they play with such toys, pitting heroic space-refugee Autobots up against evil space-invaders the Decepticons, and it's these (admittedly childish) fantasies that Bay's movies have turned into live-action spectaculars with photo-real CGI animation. A similar process is also true of thematic readings from comicbooks such as *The Incredible Hulk*. The progressive developments of CGI have unleashed the production of such fantastic and often playful images from pure imagination into magnificently visual epics, made possible by today's ongoing digital revolution of cinema with higher degrees of realism.

The editing of *Hulk* generally follows a distinctive pattern of cutting and emphasising to clarify or illuminate, not obfuscate details simply to generate a mystique. Bruce's blackout in the cabin is fully dramatised by a closing iris/circle-in effect that centres on his face. It is an old-fashioned technique that dates back to silent movies, but it scores a keen emotional relevance in this scene, as it shows that darkness is closing in upon Bruce in more ways than one.

32

CHAPTER TWO:
CHARACTERS & COLOURS

Many characters in the monthly serials of Marvel Comics appeared in story arcs and cross-over sagas, so regular readers had to buy various titles just to follow their ongoing stories. Later, some superheroes had their characterisations wholly revised or, in current parlance, *retconned* – subjected to storyline changes to enforce a retroactive continuity. And so they could be shunted out of, or back into, existence in their fictional worlds, as requested by a new generation of writers – who were perhaps on seasonal rotation across Marvel's ever expanding range of titles – or better to suit a new marketing strategy or editorial whimsy. It was (and it still is) a volatile field that often proved frustrating and difficult to keep track of, especially with Marvel and DC Comics in competition for readers.

Right from the start, the Hulk was a lot more than just a monster-sized novelty from Marvel. While the majority of comicbook superheroes were inherently good at fighting against villainy to promote moral order and justice, the Hulk clearly was something of a breed apart. He was one of Marvel's antiheroes. As a monster/antihero, the Hulk stands in marked contrast to the likes of the iconic Superman, and not simply as a kind of necessary evil set loose upon the whole world to generate conflict in more complex dramas and moral dilemmas, but also as a deeply philosophical exploration of devil's advocacy, which, in Hulk comicbooks, scores critical points about the banality of good.

The character's origin story was told in *The Incredible Hulk* #1 (1 May 1962), written by Stan Lee, with artwork by Jack Kirby. This issue is reprinted alongside several other tales, by various writers and artists, in the graphic novel *Marvel Platinum: the Definitive Incredible Hulk* (Panini, 2008), which includes several excellent adventures detailing the history of the Hulk throughout major developments of the character spanning nearly 40 years.

Like the TV pilot of *The Incredible Hulk*, Ang Lee's movie begins with a lengthy montage. However, whereas the intro to the feature-length television origin story dealt only with Banner's dream about the loss of his wife, the beginning of *Hulk* reinvents the man, the source of the monster's power, and redefines the scientist's secret family backstory. Besides the CGI star, there are four principal characters, plus a doomed interloper, in *Hulk* …

Bruce

'When Bruce is Bruce, it's basically the Hulk using Bruce as a camouflage … when the Hulk is the Hulk, it's actually Bruce using the Hulk as camouflage.'

– Eric Bana, interviewed in
Hulk: The Official Souvenir Movie Magazine
(Titan Publishing, summer 2003)

An early scene in *Hulk* sees happy baby Bruce watching his mother, Edith, who is outside in the garden. Little Bruce is laughing in delight and – in retrospect – it is the kind of simple human emotion that Bruce loses by suppressing his feelings after he's orphaned by the family's tragedy. While treating Bruce for a minor injury, Edith notices that her son's arms and legs display a rash of sickly colour, and she frets that 'he's just so bottled up.'

Playing with stuffed toys – a green dinosaur and a somewhat doggy looking teddy – the four-year-old Bruce casually mocks his quarrelling parents, and puppeteers his toys into fighting each other, in a blurry, slow-motion and pixilated display. This amusingly foreshadows the action sequence where the Hulk fights against a trio of mutant dogs. As Ang Lee explains, during his director's commentary on Universal's Blu-ray release (2008): 'Bruce Banner's dream is Hulk's reality.'

When the teenage Bruce (Mike Erwin) wakes up from his recurring nightmare, he's comforted by his foster mother Mrs Monica Krenzler (Celia Weston). As he is preparing to leave home for college, the caring Mrs Krenzler tells him that she believes he will become a scientist and that he has 'a greatness inside' him. And she asserts, prophetically as it turns out: 'Someday you're gonna share it with the whole world.'

The superbly economical narrative in these scenes presents not only all the essential information we need to understand the seemingly cursed Banner, but also inventively foretells many of the movie's plot beats and events in clues that can be decrypted by repeat viewings. As *Hulk* focuses upon analogies of rebirth, it is apt that the movie begins with a backstory sketch of Bruce's birth and childhood.

The adult but emotionally immature Bruce Krenzler, alias Banner (Eric Bana, who played a US soldier in Ridley Scott's docudrama movie *Black Hawk Down*, 2001), is a perpetually worried introvert who is quite prone to ultimately distracting reminiscences, and succumbs very easily to paranoia due to his recurring nightmares concerning buried memories of a childhood trauma.

At the Berkeley Nuclear Biotechnology Institute labs, Betty suggests that Bruce should help with a presentation: 'Start talking about microbes and nano-meds, and you sound almost passionate.' There's an awkward pause, then Betty apologises for needling Bruce, as they both recognise the discomfort and tension between them but have very different ways of dealing with how it affects their professional partnership.

Betty's past relationship with Bruce is explored in a flashback where she tells him about a dream: 'I think it's my first memory.' Aged about two, she recalls being left alone, crying in a roadside ice-cream parlour, while a green mushroom cloud rises up from a gamma bomb explosion on the horizon. It is a powerful and haunting nuclear tableau that recalls the US postwar government's civil defence propaganda; a political campaign of the Cold War era whose archive movies were cleverly satirised in the documentary horror *The Atomic Café* (1982).

An even more psychologically disturbing shot featuring little Betty (Rhiannon Leigh Wryn, who went on to star in Robert Shaye's fantasy *The Last Mimzy*, 2007), shows her being picked up by the adult Bruce, who grimaces menacingly, foreshadowing the Hulk picking up the adult Betty in a later scene. Stepping back from this reflective level of narrative, out of Betty's remembered dream, we return to Bruce's reminiscence as he assures her: 'You know I'd never hurt you.' The storyline exits this double-layered memory and reverie sequence, but it has successfully drawn us into the past lives of the lead characters.

Bruce's recurring nightmares, which usually end with a bedroom door opening, eventually reveal a green figure lurking in the shadows beyond it. In a steady build-up of narrative tensions, this image marks the figurative approach of the Hulk. These anxiety dreams are prompted, in part, by the increasing workaday pressures upon Bruce.

He is not interested in any military applications of the work on nano-meds, and he counters the visiting Talbot's super-soldier suggestion, calmly explaining: 'That's not what we're doing here. We're doing the basic science, for everyone.' This pacifist aspect of Bruce's philosophy informs the Hulk's reluctance to fight unless provoked. Talbot cannot leave without issuing a thinly-veiled threat, against Bruce and (by implication) against Betty, too. It is a pivotal scene, firmly establishing the opposing moral positions of protagonist Bruce versus antagonist Talbot. Talbot provokes Bruce's instinctive hostility because Bruce sees him as a threat to the ethical purity of the lab's nanotech research, and also mistakenly as his obvious rival for Betty's affections.

Following the lab accident, there's a solidly emotional depth to the performances of both Bana and Nolte when Bruce meets ex-convict David. This rather intimate little reunion scene is utterly confusing for Bruce, as the unkempt stranger who claims to be his father says that Bruce is not only his 'physical son', but *the child of his mind*, too … Bruce maintains a cagey silence, as if in denial of the truth, even when David's bedside manner invades Bruce's personal space. David tries to warn Bruce about Betty and the danger that her father represents, but Bruce reacts angrily, and so David leaves with the parting remark: 'We're gonna have to watch that temper of yours.'

Bruce slowly begins to understand the psychological impact of how trauma buried in his lost childhood has resulted in a repressive personality in adulthood. His comment about losing all control and liking it (the line used as a voiceover for the *Hulk* teaser trailer), when he changes into the Hulk, is not an indicator of his dark side, it's a revelation of clarity – of a light in the darkness – and a glimpse of the memories that Bruce has kept hidden since infancy. There is a potent irony in the way that his past is revealed by his transformations into the Hulk.

The man is, almost literally, his own worst enemy. His unbreakable habit of retreating into himself is due to external/social pressures just as much as it is caused by a subconscious repression of his feelings. When Bruce receives a fateful message from Betty about her father's suspicions, his anxious state associates her warning with gamma-bomb memory-dreams, and when Betty says that she thinks *they* (the military-industrial complex, as represented by Ross and Talbot) 'are planning something', more vague memories and clues to the mystery of his mother's death resurface. Even before his change into the Hulk, Bruce becomes severely agitated, feeling tricked by circumstances and trapped in a fugue between himself and his personal demons.

Is Bruce's future predestined or damned? In the novelisation, Betty begs her dad: 'Don't punish the son for the sins of the father.' (Page 249, *Hulk* by Peter David, Boxtree, 2003.) Ang Lee's movie has more subtlety in outlining the lack of any understanding between Ross and his daughter about Bruce's nature, but Betty's argument amounts to the same pleading for compassion.

Betty

'This woman [Betty] is struggling for something really sacred and pure, in a world that's so superficial and flat.'

– Jennifer Connelly, interviewed in
Hulk: The Official Souvenir Movie Magazine
(Titan Publishing, summer 2003)

In the original comicbook, Betty consoles Banner when he's accosted by Ross, who is impatient for the gamma bomb test countdown to begin. Betty is more respectful of scientific pioneers, and clearly sympathetic to anyone facing her father's blustering ego. For the 21st Century updating of the story, it makes good sense that Betty should be a scientist herself. So, in Ang Lee's movie she is nerdy Bruce's colleague and ex-girlfriend, biophysicist Dr Elizabeth 'Betty' Ross (Jennifer

Connelly, who portrayed the schizophrenic mathematician's wife in Ron Howard's *A Beautiful Mind*, 2001).

Career-minded and thoroughly independent, Betty finds herself still attracted to Bruce, but his psychological problems strained their romance, and she found him initially fascinating but frustrating. And yet her feelings for Bruce are never far from the surface. Although Bruce wakes up from the potentially lethal gamma-sphere accident, and says that he feels fine, Betty is tearfully distraught, having feared she might have had to watch him die. Connelly is particularly adept at playing vulnerable characters with depths of conviction and hidden strengths, and her scenes opposite Bana gift *Hulk* with a solid foundation of emotional developments for the fantastical dramas.

While leaving work, Betty meets the new night-shift caretaker, David, and his lurking appearance is a rather ominous turn of events for all concerned. This encounter in *Hulk* harks back to 13-year-old TV movie *The Death of the Incredible Hulk*, which featured Bill Bixby's David Banner employed under the false name of David Bellamy, who takes a job as a maintenance worker at government science lab Genecore, where he sneakily gains access to another scientist's research in an attempt to find a cure to prevent his Hulk transformations. The comicbook trivia in *The Death of the Incredible Hulk* includes a Genecore security guard named Betty, so this quiet scene of Connelly's Betty meeting Nolte's David in Ang Lee's movie pays tribute to Bixby's enduring legacy.

In *Hulk*, when Betty meets her father at the officer's club restaurant of the military base overlooking San Francisco bay, he wants to warn her about Bruce. Of course, Ross is 'not at liberty to disclose ...' any details, and they are both painfully aware of how this cliché about official state secrets divides them, philosophically, emotionally, and politically, as it demonstrates their opposing positions on matters of social conscience. Betty is reduced to frustrated tears by this other emotionally-distant man in her life. Their father and daughter relationship is clearly no better than the broken bonds of father and son between Bruce and David. What little rapport Betty shares with Bruce is seemingly based upon mutual feelings of neglect/abandonment by their parents.

In the comicbook, Betty is a less grounded and more whimsically inclined character. At her father's residence, a troubled Betty confides her musings about Bruce to her off-duty dad: 'I feel as though we're on the brink of some fantastic unimaginable adventure!' (*The Incredible Hulk* #1, page 19). This 1960s version of Betty is also more fragile. When she first meets the monster, she is reflecting on the day's events and wondering aloud: 'Perhaps I can tell myself it was all a dream – there is no Hulk!' Caught by surprise, she faints upon facing the Hulk when he approaches her. Although this scene in the comicbook obviously alludes to *Beauty and the Beast*, that genre reference only works for *Hulk* in a different context.

For the movie, Betty meets the monster when he is standing in bushes, camouflaged by the greenery surrounding a cabin in the woods. There is a curious momentary impulse for weird farce when she looks up at the almost motionless giant creature and easily recognises Bruce. For a comicbook story, this is an ironic anomaly. Most superhero characters, such as DC's Batman and Marvel's Spider-Man, maintain their secret identities with a costume and a mask. Superman is distinguished from his alter-ego, Clark Kent, when the newspaper reporter simply takes off his spectacles and changes his behaviour.

In this movie version of the comicbook, everyone knows (well, eventually they will!) that Bruce is the Hulk. The fact that Betty can recognise Bruce as the Hulk is not a very difficult concept to accept if we consider the way our brains perceive human faces. It is, after all, our primary method of identifying others. (I cannot always remember names, but I rarely forget a face.)

Unlike the comicbook's Betty, our heroine in *Hulk* does not faint on sight of the creature. She acts like the Hulk is just a big kid to her. His massive presence in the forest, just standing there and looking a bit lost, prompts her maternal feelings, and Betty's unflustered manner brings out the *gentle giant* aspect of the Hulk's largely innocent persona. There is an appealing fairytale moment, with its homage to the *Beauty and the Beast* imagery of *King Kong*, as the Hulk picks Betty up, and puts her inside the car, when he senses an approaching danger. This recalls Betty's dream about her earliest memory, where the adult Bruce was there, in the ice-cream parlour, to pick her up when she was a frightened little girl. Was Betty's dream a kind of premonition?

While the Hulk is fighting the dogs, Betty is trapped inside her car. She is quite terrified, throughout the nightmarish ordeal, but does not scream in panic. She gasps in shock or shouts in alarm, but *Hulk*'s Betty never once succumbs to hysteria. No wonder a needy neurotic like Bruce believes that she is a heroine worth fighting for.

In a genre context of powerful conflicts between rationalistic science and militaristic rage, with the love of a proverbial good woman providing a source of redemption for a deeply troubled hero, what this movie achieves in constructing Betty's character as a positive influence upon the duality of Bruce and the Hulk is a very shrewd compilation of traditional fantasy and modern SF tropes, adding considerable appeal to the popular mythology.

David

'You have this comicbook level, but then you have mythic proportions to it … which is archetypal, primal stuff.'

– Nick Nolte, interviewed in
Hulk: The Official Souvenir Movie Magazine
(Titan Publishing, summer 2003)

Only David Banner's name is drawn from the live-action TV series. His character comes, at least in part, from Brian David Banner, Bruce's psychotically abusive father in a retconned comicbook timeline, started by Mike Mignola and Bill Mantlo in *The Incredible Hulk* #312 (Marvel, October 1985). However, in Ang Lee's *Hulk*, David is a significantly different brand of demented genius from Brian as, for a start, Brian gained no super-powers.

In the title sequence of *Hulk*, we see the young David (Paul Kersey) in his laboratory. Although his workspace lacks any gothic paraphernalia (common to many screen adaptations of *Frankenstein*), David's egotistical notes reveal a fanatical personality in tune with the subgenre staple of a mad scientist: 'I intend to achieve human regeneration,' he writes, adding the ominous exclamation, 'regeneration is immortality!', as he prepares to begin tests on primates. Undeterred by early failure, David perseveres, but his stubborn nature drives him to ignore the Presidential diktat that forbids human testing, and he recklessly injects himself with an experimental compound. He does not regret his decision, but notes there are 'hints of genetic modification', when the unsuspecting Mrs Edith Banner (Carla Buono) declares that she is pregnant.

At home, abusive father David draws blood from his young son's arm, and notes that lab results confirm his 'worst fears', but he concludes that he wants to 'find a cure' for whatever is wrong with the abnormally impassive Bruce. Decades later, David conducts experiments at home in his makeshift lab, turning a rat into a giant green rodent, and his pet dogs into deadly monsters. He seems, at times, to be the epitome of that genre cliché – the obsessive genius, with many of the very worst human flaws, especially arrogance. After 30 years' imprisonment, David (Nick Nolte, who had played a gambler in Neil Jordan's crime drama *The Good Thief*, 2002), is released, and finds work as a caretaker at the lab where Bruce and Betty work. His tackling of the menial job without any pride or vague concerns over his lowly position reveals the secretive and utterly manipulative nature of David's increasingly sinister and aloof mentality.

At David's house, where Betty admits that her own father is holding Bruce in military custody, David berates her, trying to displace some of his own guilt onto her, saying in a haughty tone: 'How little you understand, Miss Ross, and how dangerous your ignorance has become.' Concealing his true motive, David stoops to invading Betty's personal space, just as he did with Bruce in the infirmary. What seems like sexual harassment is merely a ploy by David to unnerve Betty so that he can steal from her. Escaping from the atmosphere of unsubtle hostility, Betty is evidently too keen to get away from such a creepy old man to bother about what he's taken from her, or why.

Betty's final encounter with David sees him waiting for her, claiming that he is ready to turn himself in peacefully. David makes it clear that he is not asking for sympathy but appealing to her for help so that he can see his son, 'for one last time.' It sounds like a reasonable request from a summarily condemned man, but the manipulative David is only permitting himself to be taken into custody for his own ends. David starts ranting about giving men 'the power to go beyond god's boundaries' in a commentary about secularism and science that is also another direct reference to *Frankenstein* – who proclaimed: 'I know what it feels like to be God!' David rambles on (as if he assumes Betty will understand, if not relate) about his wife wanting a baby, while at that very moment Bruce is locked inside a hi-tech *womb* all ready for another rebirth as the Hulk. Echoing the melancholy speeches of all those crazy scientists in 20th Century sci-fi movies, David laments: 'I was curious, and that was my downfall.'

In the movie's finale, David rants and raves like a man possessed – and indeed he is. Nolte is portraying a thoroughly obsessed scientist with a god complex, a man whose own genius led him so far astray that he was locked away for half a lifetime. When he is finally released back into a different world, he simply abuses any newfound knowledge to experiment upon himself, yet again, and so acquires bizarre super-powers. Is Nolte playing David as a megalomaniac loony? Of course he is! He is over-the-top by necessity for his character's development in a comicbook narrative, but he is creepy and scary and quite funny all at the same time. This is a shrewdly conceived performance for such a difficult and complex role.

ROSS

'The Hulk is something that's in all of us, this black/white thing within our character'

> – Sam Elliott, interviewed in
> *Hulk: The Official Souvenir Movie Magazine*
> (Titan Publishing, summer 2003)

Betty's father appears in the very first dialogue scene of *Hulk*'s overture sequence, which establishes the movie's backstory elements begun in the montage prologue. US army Captain

Ross (Todd Tesen) argues with David about advanced work on a 'super-immune response' for military purposes. In the present day, he's four-star General Thaddeus 'Thunderbolt' Ross (Sam Elliott, who played a sergeant-major in Vietnam War movie *We Were Soldiers*, 2002), running the secretive – and fictional – Joint Tactical Force West organisation's base.

In the scene where Betty hurries away from the restaurant table, leaving her father to dine alone, Ross just sits there, unwilling or simply unable to abandon his military bearing and stoical demeanour to show much honest affection for his daughter. It is a perfectly judged scene in this movie's heartfelt relationship dramas, where the cast never slip into unconvincing hysteria or the mawkishness of TV soap opera.

When Ross questions Bruce about his father David, Bruce denies having any memory of his own early childhood. Ross cannot believe that Bruce has blanked out so much of his past, and he is menacing when he admits to putting Bruce's father in prison, and openly threatens Bruce's career prospects while telling him in no uncertain terms to keep away from Betty. Ross embodies an intolerance for any weakness that brings him to a quiet respect for the Hulk, whom he code-names 'Angry Man', but no admiration for Bruce's genius whatsoever. On the streets of San Francisco, when Betty's presence tames the Hulk so that he turns back into Bruce, Ross is just as helpless as any bystander. Although he can grudgingly acknowledge his daughter's exceptional courage, this only prompts him to recognise his own failings, as a father and as a man.

As the unconscious Bruce is despatched into the bowels of

the military hive called Desert Base, a worried Betty asks her father: 'How long are you gonna keep him sedated?' And Ross answers, brusquely: 'For the rest of his natural life, if I have to.' He adds, as if by way of explaining his motives: 'You can trust me to do what I think is right, not what you think you want,' which reveals the sheer audacity and fearsome scale of the old soldier's domineering arrogance.

Ross is furious when he learns that Talbot has gained all control of studying the Hulk. The NSA (National Security Agency) have handed the threat assessment to political player Talbot because of his connection to the supposedly private company Atheon. This is a hint of the government conspiracy that is revealed in the novelisation. Although he remains in charge of Desert Base, Ross receives new orders, and he rants, in Betty's presence, that it's all about the power of big money, and that any human tragedy is just 'collateral damage'. This disempowerment is alarming for Ross and exposes his flawed humanity more clearly. Despite the man's risibly egotistical pride, he becomes a wholly sympathetic character in this moment. When Ross orders a gamma-charge air strike, as the only viable nuclear option, against the Hulk and his father at Pear Lake, it is because Ross is brimming with remorse over his complete failure to use military force to contain the situation. In the movie, he insists, repeatedly, that he will 'get to the bottom' of the vexing Krenzler/Banner situation, but in the end it is the Hulk that exposes all of Ross's secrets and flaws.

Elliott is on great acting form throughout *Hulk*. He portrays Ross as menacingly obsessed with protecting his daughter whether she likes it or not, and he glowers with utter contempt over any seemingly unpatriotic, or maverick, geniuses like David and Bruce. Elliott's grizzled appearance and gruff voice make him the epitome of the tough Hollywood cowboy, and he excels in iconic Western roles, like that of Virgil Earp in *Tombstone* (1993). After *Hulk*, he went on to play a former cowboy vigilante in the supernatural superhero movie *Ghost Rider* (2007), but Ross remains his strongest performance to date. In a curious bit of coincidental trivia, Elliott is married to actress Katherine Ross.

Talbot

'To me it's like the purest form of acting and imagination.'

– Josh Lucas, interviewed in
Hulk: The Official Souvenir Movie Magazine
(Titan Publishing, summer 2003)

The initial villain of *Hulk* is Glenn Talbot (blue-eyed blond Josh Lucas, who starred opposite Christian Bale in Mary Harron's *American Psycho*, 2000), an ambitious ex-soldier who has become a corporate pinstripe for defence contractor Atheon. When Talbot greets Betty in the Berkeley Institute, he admits that he still works with her father, but claims to run all the labs on the army base. Talbot knows Betty from her college days. It is not made clear in the movie how close they were but, in the novelisation, author Peter David explores Betty's teenage years and reveals that Talbot was the only boyfriend Betty ever had that her father approved of. Talbot is far more interested in her research project now, and he is offering big money – with patent shares – if she will sign up with Atheon, but Betty flatly rejects this allegorically Faustian pact when he infers that Atheon plans to acquire her and Bruce's nanotech research strictly for military purposes.

Talbot warns Bruce about plans for a corporate takeover by Atheon, revealing that the idea for the healing power of nano-meds is 'dynamite', and Talbot's mindset envisions a lucrative possibility of 'GIs embedded with technology that makes them instantly repairable on the battlefield.' Talbot's capitalist scheming and his viewpoint of using nanotech research not for saving civilian lives and enhancing public health but for military purposes, is *Hulk*'s primary allusion to modern America's military-industrial complex.

When the belligerent Talbot barges into Bruce's house, he is angry because Ross is thwarting his capitalist schemes to exploit the research into nano-medical applications, and he wrongly blames Bruce for all of his business troubles. Talbot's character flaws are that he overvalues his career ambitions while underestimating his moral opponents, including Bruce, but particularly his most fearsome adversary the Hulk.

Palette

Using traditional comicbook design, with simple layouts of rectangular boxes and white borders, *The Incredible Hulk* #1 seems basic compared with the overlapping panels and stylised sequential artwork of today's rather more sophisticated graphic novels. But Kirby's illustrative storytelling is now recognised and celebrated as iconic pop art, and his work was an unparalleled influence upon the subsequent output of Marvel Comics and the comicbook medium in general.

However, in the case of the Hulk, the four-colour printings suffered from a technical difficulty. The first version of the character was supposed to be grey-skinned, but mostly came out in various shades of blue. This is a distraction, but nothing more than that, and the comic's presentation of its storyline remains eminently readable today, because of the elegant simplicity of Kirby's art. As Stan Lee recounts the anecdote (in the DVD extras of *Hulk*), which has long since passed into legend, the editorial decision to make the Hulk green-skinned was taken on an almost purely arbitrary basis. It was simply because there were fewer green coloured characters in superhero comics at that time.

For the live-action TV series, although 'the colour of rage is red' – as pilot episode director Johnson says in his DVD commentary – a suggestion to make the Hulk a red-skinned giant was overruled by others, including Johnson's friend Stan Lee. In the resulting characterisation for a primetime genre drama, the Hulk was portrayed by champion bodybuilder Lou Ferrigno, who was six foot four inches tall, weighed approx 250 lbs and had 26-inch round biceps: the 'largest arms in the world' (Johnson's DVD commentary). A couple of shots left in the TV pilot feature Johnson's first choice of actor, Richard Kiel, as the Hulk, but it was decided that Ferrigno's remarkable physique was a far better asset to the show than the greater height of the seven foot two inches tall Kiel – still best known for playing a henchman named 'Jaws' in the James Bond movies *The Spy Who Loved Me* (1977) and *Moonraker* (1979). Ferrigno's great physical presence made the Hulk an endearing character throughout the series and its subsequent revival movies. The importance of Johnson's TV version as an influence upon Ang Lee's *Hulk* cannot be overstated. Much about the antihero character is different in the movie, but it is the colourful tone combined with a philosophical approach carried over from TV to cinema that is a vital part of *Hulk*'s success.

For the Hulk's first appearance in the movie, he is partly grey, which is used as an interim signifier in the movie's colour scheme. During the battle with the dogs, the greener and meaner Hulk loses much of the ragged fabric of what is left of Bruce's grey boxer shorts. We will see the comicbook Hulk's classic purple trousers in other scenes. Shades of green and purple recur throughout the movie. They are used as lighting to give interior scenes a dramatic emphasis, and for colourful thematic accents of jade and violet that appear frequently in décor, props and furnishings. During many of the transitional moments between live-action sequences, there are fluidic swirls and macroscopic views, often generated by digital effects; right up until the movie's closing fade-out to a plain green screen.

As the unconscious Bruce is securely transported into the military bunker complex, the live-action switches into a colour-coded wire-frame graphic of Desert Base before a digital dissolve to an introductory scene for the movie's biggest set: the main hall, which has a four-colour décor brightening up what could have been just a rather dull concrete burrow of manmade caverns. This affectionate tribute to the basic palette of comicbooks recalls a similarly retro affectation used for the designer stylings of Warren Beatty's pulp adventure *Dick Tracy* (1990).

Perceptions

The best special effects go unnoticed but, nowadays, genre filmmaking requires visuals of unreality that cannot possibly be anything else but effects work, so they are easily identifiable as fake. For such visual effects to work in favour of the storytelling in movies requires considerable skills, both artistic and technological, on the part of filmmakers, to overcome implausibilities in their scenarios. However, it also requires something from viewers: the willing suspension of disbelief.

Everybody is capable of this act. We all do it on an everyday basis with our money, because currencies are actually nothing more than a *consensual reality* wherein we all choose to agree that bits of printed paper (promissory banknotes are regarded as more than just IOUs) and coins have more than their intrinsic value.

In terms of watching movies, it is about abandoning any cynicism to engage fully with the story unfolding on a projection screen or through the haunted window of a TV set. Acceptance by viewers of traditional types of special visual effects depends, mostly, upon a seamless combination and interactivity between the real physical world of sets and locations and the fake or imaginary elements achieved via camera trickery. Or, as in the case of the Hulk character, a computer animation based in part upon a motion-capture performance.

Our current nostalgia for 20th Century fantasy movies with stop-motion animation by the likes of Ray Harryhausen is no doubt informed by genuine respect for such artistry. However, it is often the case with 21st Century movies that CGI attracts undue criticism, and many frequently derisive comments, perhaps due to the viewer's failed attempts to cross the 'uncanny valley' – a term coined in 1970 by Japanese robotics expert Masahiro Mori. A pioneering theory about our interactions with *humanoid* creations, the uncanny valley posits a negative emotional reaction (usually of revulsion) when an observer confronts a facsimile of humanity. The closer to being indistinguishable-from-human that any robot or 3D photo-real animated figure becomes, the stronger our instinctive and paradoxical response of rejection to its human likeness becomes. A psychological hurdle, this can be linked to our existential feelings about mortality and questions of human identity, and the lack of empathy that SF writer Philip K Dick asserted would be a primary distinguishing characteristic between the *android* and the authentically human.

Perceptual problems aside, the daunting task of *Hulk's* visual effects supervisor, Dennis Muren, at the Lucasfilm subsidiary company Industrial Light & Magic (ILM), was to achieve the first ever CGI character that is a movie star – in the sense of being a genuinely sympathetic protagonist with some degree of recognisably authentic humanity instead of simply a cartoon figure – such as Shrek, appearing in a franchised series of movies (2001-2010) by Dreamworks Animation.

A fairytale character created by the cartoonist and author William Steig, Shrek is a green blobby creature that's only vaguely human in shape. *Shrek* is a farce set in a comedic land of absurd caricatures, and the movies still rely upon the principles of anthropomorphism for any success. The effectiveness of anthropomorphism depends upon viewers to attribute human characteristics to the obviously non-human, and it is what makes so many cartoon animals or toys appealing to children (and adults). For *Hulk*, the CGI creators aimed far beyond that by skilfully combining a unique photo-real animated character with a wide range of live-action scenes.

Earlier attempts to create a fully-CG character, such as Gollum, the corrupted hobbit seen in Peter Jackson's highly ambitious live-action epic *The Lord of the Rings* trilogy (2001-2003), proved effective in generating sympathy from attentive viewers. Whenever I watch the scenes of Gollum arguing with his own ego in those movies, it is almost impossible not to be caught up in the Tolkien character's moral dilemma. And yet, Gollum had the distinct advantage of dialogue (voiced by Andy Serkis) to help explore his schizoid character, with all the emotion that a human voice can evoke, whereas the Hulk has (almost) nothing to say in Ang Lee's movie, so the burden is upon the CGI work to create a character via persuasive facial expressions and convincing body language. The artists at ILM are wholly successful on every level, and this is what makes *Hulk* such a marvellous achievement and a milestone in the history of cinema fantastique.

In the end, of course, it is pointless to criticise the Hulk for being an all-CGI creation, because the character is based closely upon comicbook drawings of an outlandish creature. Any failure to appreciate the Hulk as a fully-rounded character may not be the fault of the filmmakers. Viewers need only permit themselves to allow the computer-generated Hulk to appear convincingly *real* within the context of a spectacular action movie, and in the movie's serious dramas of human relationships, for *Hulk* to succeed as great entertainment. Using the very latest CGI developments to create sympathetic characters was perfectly demonstrated in Rupert Wyatt's *Rise of the Planet of the Apes* (2011), where the super-intelligent chimpanzee named Caesar, based on the motion-capture scans of virtual role-play by Andy Serkis, gives a genuinely dramatic performance that is superior to those of some of the human cast.

The main points here are: first, the Hulk is more than adequately realised on screen as a huge, green-skinned monster and, secondly, that he (certainly not *it*) is an excellently portrayed character cursed with the fiercely emotional turmoil of inner conflicts while suffering through tragic failings. The Hulk is the most unguardedly *human* character in Ang Lee's movie.

CHAPTER THREE:
TRANSFORMATIONS:
EVERYTHING'S GREEN

The most striking transformation found in *Hulk* is the winning combination of elements from the original comicbook and the television adaptation, so it is appropriate to consider the background of the small screen version to appreciate how it diverged significantly from the comicbook source, and how such creativity in the telefantasy industry fed the development of Ang Lee's big screen masterwork.

There were some cartoon series featuring the Hulk, first in 1966 as part of *The Marvel Super Heroes*, but adapting the unusual character into a live-action drama presented many daunting challenges. Developed for Universal Studios by Kenneth Johnson, *The Incredible Hulk* (1978-1982) was a laudable attempt to produce something very different from the other superhero shows on TV. Other live-action adaptations of the same era include *The Amazing Spider-Man* (1977-1979); Philip DeGuere's colourful tele-movie *Dr Strange* (1978) – about Marvel's sorcerer supreme, who battles occult evil forces from other supernatural dimensions; and Rod Holcomb's updated version of *Captain America*, plus prompt sequel *Captain America II: Death Too Soon* (both 1979). All of these tried to approximate the super-powers of their heroes just as they appeared on comicbook pages, garish costumes and all. While they might, charitably, be viewed as modestly successful in their aims – for the decade in which they were created – if we also take into account the constraints of TV budgets for stunts and various special effects, none of them can be viewed as very much more than a frivolous timewaster by today's usually higher standards of superhero movies.

Kenneth Johnson enjoyed a rather illustrious career in US television. Before working on *The Incredible Hulk*, his popular action shows included *The Six Million Dollar Man* (1975-1976) and its spin-off series *The Bionic Woman* (1976-1978). Like the protagonists of Monty Berman's groundbreaking TV series *The Champions* (1968-1969), that bionic duo were portrayed as plain-clothes superheroes, fighting criminals and other threats to society in real world settings. They could be easily identified as telefantasy programmes – not unlike *The Man from Atlantis* (1977-1978) and Steven Bochco's *The Invisible Man* (1975-1976) – and would later be categorised as TV sci-fi alongside such techno-fetishistic programmes as Donald Bellisario's *Airwolf* (1984-1986), about a super-helicopter, Glen A Larson's *Knight Rider* (1982-1986), featuring a talking gadget–car, and *Street Hawk* (1985), with its eponymous hero on a hi-tech motorcycle.

Against this background of successful plain-clothes superheroes, Johnson opted to write *The Incredible Hulk* as a primetime drama with a sympathetic and engaging protagonist instead of the more outlandish antihero of Marvel's comics. Rationalising the need for an origin scenario that was achievable on a TV budget – '$1.3 or 1.4 million' according to Johnson's audio commentary track on the DVD (Universal, 2003) – the 90-minute pilot episode and its subsequent series significantly reduced the Hulk's super-powers. This was a crucial decision to ensure the show could be produced as episodic drama from limited resources.

The Incredible Hulk on TV stars Bill Bixby as Dr David Bruce Banner. The forename David was chosen instead of Bruce to break a tiresomely familiar pattern of alliteration for the names of comicbook characters (like Peter Parker, alias Spider-Man; Reed Richards – Mr Fantastic; Scott Summers – Cyclops in the X-Men; Dr Stephen Strange, etc).

Bill Bixby had previously starred in Bruce Lansbury's TV series *The Magician* (1973-1974), and he was a splendid actor, so talented when it came to portrayals of melancholy and yet compassionate heroes who all seem to carry the burden of wisdom on their shoulders. In *The Incredible Hulk*, he explores a terribly lonely humanity that makes him perhaps the most tragic hero in television history.

The series featured a tinkling piano tune, entitled 'The Lonely Man'. It was a poignant refrain by Joseph Harnell. A deceptively simple melody, it's used economically in the show to underline particularly heartrending moments of sorrow for the troubled protagonist. It's one the finest pieces of commercial music I have ever heard, and remains one of the most memorable and effective TV show themes ever composed.

Bixby's characterisation of Banner was partly inspired by David Janssen's heroic role as Dr Richard Kimble in TV drama *The Fugitive* (1963-1967), created by Roy Huggins. In that show, Kimble is wrongly accused of murdering his wife, but escapes from police custody and goes on the run from the authorities, represented by his regular pursuer, Lieutenant Philip Gerard (Barry Morse). Kimble is innocent of the crime, and claims a one-armed thug was the actual killer. As a wanted man, Kimble has to conceal his identity, while travelling between cities and small towns, often risking his life to help other people in trouble. For *The Incredible Hulk* TV show, Banner is also forced to adopt a drifter's lifestyle, always on the move, unable to settle down. And he is normally unwilling to trust anyone with his dark secret, or even give his real name. Using the format of *The Fugitive* as the major inspiration for the protagonist's episodic adventures was one of Johnson's best choices for his television adaptation of the comicbook scenario.

Explained by the voiceover introduction that would be used for all of the TV episodes, the genre element hinged upon the phrase: 'a startling metamorphosis occurs.' Banner's eyes turn albino white, his shirt is torn apart by the flexing of bulked-up muscles, his shoes burst at the seams, and he becomes the Hulk; played by Lou Ferrigno, with a bushy wig over the protrusions of a prosthetic forehead, mono-brow, and full-body green greasepaint. A green spotlight and a series of overlapping dissolves, with each shot showing interim stages of special make-up, are used to depict Banner changing into the Hulk, while an eerie choral sound provides a fitting accompaniment. Later in the TV series, the uncanny chorus would be used as a sound cue, usually to immediately follow a close-up shot of the albino eyes effect (achieved through contact lenses that, reportedly, Bixby loathed wearing because they were so painful), while the transformation occurred off-screen, thus saving the production money on recreating and restaging the sequence of special make-up dissolves. Long before the advent of digital morphing via computer-generated animation (CGI), such camera trickery was common practice for similar transformations in that era's cinema and TV.

If the comicbook origin story was inspired, in part, by fears about nuclear weapons and the effects of radiation, the TV adaptation (first broadcast on 26 May 1978 in the UK, a full 16 years after issue #1 of the comicbook was published) is, primarily, a lot more concerned with DNA mutations and the possibilities of genetic engineering. Banner is a scientist searching for a common denominator in rare cases where ordinary people perform apparently superhuman feats while they are under great stress.

It explores the many ways that common human characteristics are at odds with the manmade world, and scientific or industrial hardware often takes on an adversarial role in *The Incredible Hulk* TV series for dramas that embrace the techno-thriller subgenre but not technophobia; and these themes are also present in Ang Lee's *Hulk*.

In Johnson's TV pilot movie, when the Hulk is shot by a hunter, the creature reacts angrily, of course, disarming the man and storming off. When he turns back into Banner, the scientist finds that his gunshot wound has formed scar tissue in hours, not days, indicating that he has gained a capacity for rapid healing from his altered metabolism. The Hulk could easily have killed his attacker but leaves the man unharmed. As in the comicbook, we see the Hulk depicted as a pacifist who avoids conflict, whenever possible.

Johnson's most effective contribution to Hulk lore was his decision to have Ferrigno portray the monster as a truly innocent being, although the inspiration for this can be traced back to the Marvel comicbooks. In *The Avengers* #1 (September 1963) by Stan Lee and Jack Kirby, where Thor's half-brother Loki secretly observes the Hulk, the Norse god of mischief remarks: 'There is no evil in his heart, mankind fears him because of his awesome strength.'

The Hulk has a primitive mind and he is a creature of instinct, not intellect, so it is more effective in the context of a TV drama that the Hulk never speaks. Sometimes, the Hulk's appearances seem rather more like a problem child's tantrums than the unleashing of a dangerously violent, subhuman creature. A talking Hulk for television would probably have wrecked the characterisation of the man-monster effect, and it spoils the appeal of any screen version – as was the case in Louis Leterrier's movie *The Incredible Hulk* (2008), for which Ferrigno provided the voice (more about that reboot later).

Remember, King Kong does not speak, either, but the mythic quality of the great ape – taken from his jungle home and exposed to garish and cynical exploitation in a supposedly civilised world – was still presented on screen in the form of a fully-rounded character with a magnificently cinematic appeal and nobility. Much like the sympathetic characterisation of King Kong, the circumstances of the Hulk on television offer an expression of pathos that no words in any language could very easily or adequately communicate.

As a spin-off from that live-action telefantasy, Marvel produced 13 episodes of an animated series, also titled *The Incredible Hulk* (1982-1983), with narration by Stan Lee. That show was followed by a series of 21 cartoon episodes, again entitled *The Incredible Hulk* (1996-1997), with Lou Ferrigno providing the voice of Hulk. The final instalment of the live-action saga, *The Death of the Incredible Hulk* (1990), was directed by Bixby, who died three years later.

The Other Guise

The stunning prologue of *Hulk* runs under the opening credits for nearly four and a half minutes, continuing for another seven minutes with an overture of powerfully dramatic scenes, constructed with much symbolic foreshadowing, that guides us from the mid-1960s into the present day.

We see the younger David conducting genetic engineering experiments, and the handwritten notes about his research project are initially datelined February 1965. All of this being achieved in the 1960s means a divergent historical timeline for this movie, where the significant progress made in biotech sciences occurred many years before gene sequencing was possible in the real world. Although all of this is basically just a massive alternative-history info-dump, its introduction to the mythopoeic sci-fi world of *Hulk* benefits immensely from art-house stylisations, and skilfully avoids imposing an exposition overload upon the attentive viewer.

David's tests on marine life produce DNA exemplars from a lizard, jellyfish, sea cucumber and starfish. These four codes of life, required for producing a unique mutation, are scientific counterparts to the quartet of classic genre works (*Frankenstein*, Jekyll and Hyde, *King Kong*, *Beauty and the Beast*) that inform the Hulk mythos as its primary influences. Bruce's mutant DNA bonds with the infusion of nano-meds activated by the gamma-radiation, and the unanticipated side-effects are multiplied by emotional damage to form the prime causes of Bruce's transformation.

In a playpen, the infant Bruce (played by twins David and Michael Kronenberg) is made to cry so that his curious dad can check the boy's reaction for any stress-related signs of inherited characteristics from mutant DNA. Disturbingly, the wailing child's kicking legs exhibit green patches of skin, as evidence of genetic transmission from father to son, but: 'What has been passed on?' This scene recalls the similar fears of genetic transmission from teleportation test-subject Seth Brundle (Jeff Goldblum) to his girlfriend Veronica (Geena Davis) in David Cronenberg's excellent *The Fly* (1986) – still one of the very best genre movie remakes. However, whereas in *The Fly* the pregnant Veronica is forewarned about the possibly abnormal child she is carrying, David's poor wife Edith has no idea what her husband's research may have produced. This is a disturbing development in the movie's revision of the Hulk's origin.

Alter-Ego

Jack Kirby's cover for #1 of the comicbook has the strap-line 'The strangest man of all time!' and poses a question: 'Is he man or monster or … is he both?' While the statement is pure hyperbole, the query gets to the heart of the matter. Chapter two of the comicbook sees the Hulk evading soldiers who are searching for him. The Hulk's private thoughts – his first words in a thought-bubble rather than a speech balloon – are 'Mustn't let them find me …' (*The Incredible Hulk* #1, page seven), which informs readers that, while the Hulk is capable of great stealth for such a ponderous giant; he wants to avoid conflict and direct contact with other people.

The first hint of any superhuman change in *Hulk* comes in the post-credits scene with Bruce shaving before going to work. He is mildly perturbed by a faint glowing green tinge to his eye colour. It is a moment of suspense that was used to such good effect in the teaser trailer. During the second lab test, Bruce's and Betty's co-worker Jake Harper (Kevin Rankin) reports a damaged circuit. While they are trying to fix it, everything goes wrong at once, prompting the unprotected Bruce into a heroic action, not a suicidal choice, of shielding the terrified Harper (here, a stand-in for the young sidekick character Rick Jones from *The Incredible Hulk* #1 comicbook). Bruce blocks the deadly gamma discharge with his own body. It is a moment of crisis, not unlike the wartime myth of a soldier throwing himself on top of an enemy's grenade to save his comrades, where time becomes distorted. For this nano-nuke lab accident, Bruce's image blurs and stretches across the screen, a visualisation indicating his loss of consciousness, but it also anticipates his physical change in size later. Since we are already aware of David's and Talbot's antagonism towards

Bruce, we might wonder if one of them has actually sabotaged the gamma-sphere mechanism to disrupt an experiment.

This could be a reference to the comicbook role of Dr Banner's lab assistant Igor (actually a Soviet spy), who cunningly attempts to dispose of America's secretive genius. In *The Incredible Hulk* #1, when Dr Banner spots a trespassing teenager driving into danger on the gamma-bomb test range, Igor ensures that his superior's life is put at risk by not halting the countdown to detonation while Dr Banner hurries away to warn the boy.

At 42 minutes into the movie, the first Hulk transformation occurs. (In Peter David's novelisation, the Hulk does not first appear until nearly half-way through the book!) In the movie's storyline, the time is five minutes to midnight – a reference to the Doomsday Clock (which is maintained by scientists at the University of Chicago and is a symbolic gauge of the current global sociopolitical climate). In *Hulk*, this is marked symbolically by the breaking of Bruce's wristwatch. Any sense of time is the first thing that Bruce loses, of course.

With Bruce's face contorted in pain while his body is shuddering, this is clearly a quite agonising real-time mutation effect akin to the full-moon transfiguration in John Landis's classic horror *An American Werewolf In London* (1981), where the young protagonist David Kessler (a name close to Krenzler) changes into a wolf-man. That was an Oscar-winning special effects sequence designed by Rick Baker. Here, superior visuals created by ILM present a similarly groundbreaking makeover from a man into a unique monster. The nine-foot Hulk lumbers down a campus corridor, roaring with manic rage as he begins smashing up everything in sight like the proverbial bull in a china shop. The birth pangs of the green giant for Bruce's first transformation account for three minutes of mayhem in the science block. Perhaps this sequence in *Hulk* also honours the destruction caused by those little green monsters set loose in the gene-splicing labs of Dr Catheter (Christopher Lee, who portrayed Frankenstein's monster for Hammer's 1957 movie) of Joe Dante's comedy *Gremlins 2: The New Batch* (1990).

Savage Night

Following Betty's visit to his house, we see David using her scarf as a scent exemplar for his mutant dogs – which are heard snarling but are visible only as enormous shadows beyond the 12-foot high fence in his back yard. 'Go! Go get her! And let nothing stand in your way!' he bellows. Here, David is less like a modern-day Frankenstein, and much closer – in genre terms – to the mad scientist who experiments on animals in H G Wells' *The Island of Doctor Moreau* (1896), which was filmed as *The Island of Lost Souls* (1933) and remade in 1977, and again in 1996.

To infuriate Bruce, David warns him that he has used Bruce's own mutagenic DNA to transform his dogs into monsters – 'unstable, but very powerful' beasts – and they are on their way to Betty's cabin retreat in the forest park. While Bruce's first transformation into the Hulk was triggered by his overwhelmingly troubling anxieties, here it is provoked simply by his chilling fears: fear of what David has passed on

67

to him via hereditary characteristics, fear of what will happen if he changes again, and fear about his future if he cannot treat whatever is wrong with him by finding a cure. But perhaps most of all, in this scene, Bruce is afraid for Betty's immediate safety. As Talbot starts a fight, Bruce says, intensely: 'Talbot … you're making me angry.' And it's a clear reference to the signature line of dialogue from *The Incredible Hulk* TV series.

As Bruce starts turning green, we see his second change happen in a well-lit living room, in sharp contrast with those shadowy corridors of the Berkeley labs. It is such a pure, animated-comicbook style sequence, with bulging muscles swelling his arms and chest, that it briefly grants the Hulk a superbly cartoonish appeal. This almost 3D type effect evokes the Hulk's ballooning body-shape from Kirby's source drawings so perfectly that it is like few other visual effects in the movie.

Acting on Bruce's behalf, the Hulk deals roughly with the intrusive Talbot. The nine-foot giant then exits Bruce's house to confront some armed guards. A spray of 9mm rounds from H&K MP5 submachine guns bounce off the green monster's harder-than-Kevlar skin. It makes him angrier, so that he grows even bigger, rising to 12 feet as his skeleton and musculature expand, and he turns a darker hue of green. His growth spurt is depicted in a single shot, and such a bravura upscaling of the changing monster's frame showcases the impressive efforts by ILM to maintain a degree of verisimilitude in this fantastic narrative. This is the first time in the movie that the Hulk is attacked, and the madder he gets, the more dangerous he becomes – making him unstoppable, in an escalation of physical prowess that proves to have a potentially world-shaking effect in the movie's grand finale. Having broken out of custody, the Hulk leaves the night-shift guards unconscious. As he leaps out of sight, a puddle of water ripples, in homage to the similar close-up in Steven Spielberg's *Jurassic Park* (1993). Although that movie used the rippling water to signal the approach of a dinosaur, here it is like a seismic indicator of the Hulk's departure in landscape-shrinking bounds.

Partly inspired by the comicbook *The Incredible Hulk: Dogs of War* by Paul Jenkins (Marvel, 2001), the sequence with a trio of demon-eyed mutant dogs has tremendous visceral impact. At night, in the Sequoia park, it is like Arthur Conan Doyle's legendary *Hound of the Baskervilles* times three, yet these creatures are between five and six feet tall, and depicted as the most animalistic type of *werewolves* yet seen in cinema.

The Hulk fights the mastiff, the poodle and the pit bull all at once. While Betty fumbles with her car keys, the giant poodle snarls and barks at the car door's window in a satirical twist on Lewis Teague's *Cujo* (1983) – the movie in which a rabid St Bernard holds a woman (Dee Wallace) and her young son prisoner in her own car.

The Hulk is mauled in this vicious scrap. When he cannot shake off the big dogs, once their jaws clamp onto his arms, he changes tactics and bites them back. In the pit bull's final attack on the Hulk's already injured shoulder, the Hulk cannot shake the beast off. But, as if he is merely flexing his deltoid muscle, the Hulk's shoulder quickly swells up enormously, breaking the dog's jaws apart so the animal emits a fearful yelp. When the Hulk kills the dogs, they simply disintegrate into splatters, splashes and bursts of green. It appears to be a cellular instability the makes these dogs explode, recalling Bruce's and Betty's failed lab experiment upon the frog.

Panting with exhaustion, the Hulk sees that Betty is unharmed. He staggers away to the lake, where he sees his reflection in the water – a reference to *Frankenstein*, and also an image recycled from *The Incredible Hulk* on TV. The Hulk shrinks, turning into a naked and sweaty Bruce, who stumbles back toward the wrecked car, where he collapses. His memory and human consciousness are returning, slowly, but not before his lingering rage makes Betty shriek when Bruce grunts uncontrollably and grabs her neck. As the fight drains out of Bruce, Betty helps him walk to the cabin, where he recalls feverishly: 'It was like a dream … Rage… Power … And freedom.' The skirmish, which left even the Hulk exhausted, makes Bruce feel completely shattered when he returns to normal, and his full awareness re-emerges slowly from the mental fog where that harrowing violence banished his rational senses.

Betty has worked out how nano-meds and gamma radiation have combined with Bruce's altered genes to spawn the Hulk, but she wants to discuss the root cause of Bruce's transformations. Bruce comments that the nano-meds were designed only to repair physical damage, and Betty replies: 'Emotional damage can manifest physically.'

It is the fourth catalyst, in another instance of what

might be termed *Hulk*'s unwritten 'rule of fours': four genre influences, four genetic samples, four contributing factors (as above), four main characters (Bruce, Betty and their feuding fathers) and, as we shall see, four transformations of Bruce into the Hulk. There are other examples of the rule of four scattered throughout the movie, and I will get to them later.

Resistance is Change

Having taken control of Bruce's custody from Ross, Talbot is very eager to weaponise the Hulk, and he tells Bruce: 'I need your cells to trigger some chemical distress signals.' Although Talbot has already seen what happens during the change, he still wants Bruce to transform again; 'Do you mind?' he asks, sarcastically. Bruce is determined to resist, however, even if he is assaulted with electroshock. As amoral capitalist schemer and blunt-force trauma-inducer, the already injured and vengeful Talbot zaps Bruce, and muses, 'Bad science, maybe, but personally gratifying.'

Failing to break Bruce's will, Talbot puts him into a sensory isolation chamber, an immersion lab's tank that resembles a water-filled version of the pressure chamber from TV pilot movie *The Incredible Hulk*. The third transformation in *Hulk* also references sensory deprivation experiments in Ken Russell's sci-fi horror classic *Altered States* (1980). In that movie, the fanatical scientist Dr Eddie Jessup (William Hurt, who went on to play Ross in *The Incredible Hulk*, 2008), takes psychoactive drugs that he hopes will help him reach a higher level of consciousness.

What happens during Jessup's bold experimentation is that he turns into an ape-man. This is evolutionary regression (an example of atavism), which makes Jessup a primal beast when he escapes from the lab's tank and goes berserk at night, running through the streets of New York. Just like David Kessler (David Naughton) in the aforementioned *An American Werewolf In London*, Jessup's wild-man escapade ends with him waking up naked in the local zoo. There is no such embarrassing morning-after japery to be found in *Hulk*, though.

Left in charge of Bruce (and the Hulk), Talbot is not simply like a pyromaniac playing with matches. He really wants to set the world on fire. His mistreatment of Bruce is rather like putting a tinderbox on a powder-keg on top of a petrol tanker, and then leaving the gas on: 'Bingo! That must be some jumbo nightmare he just had,' observes Talbot.

But Talbot's nightmare is just beginning. As Bruce is immersed in a tank of water that's filled to capacity, the Hulk's sudden growth affects the pressure (water cannot be compressed), so a leak floods the containment bay. The 12-foot Hulk kicks his way out of the tank, and bellows with rage. Gas only makes him sneeze, but the Atheon defence crew spray him with rapidly hardening immobiliser foam that expands to fill a cylindrical corridor.

Ignoring Ross's evacuation order, Talbot fails in his last scientific effort, and his desperate solution for self-defence is to fire a grenade at his giant adversary. The armour-piercing round only bounces off the Hulk, and the shell lodges in a wall behind Talbot, who is promptly incinerated by the resulting explosion. There is a witty matte-lined freeze-frame of Talbot against a wall of flames that is highly reminiscent of comicbook splash-page artwork. The blast succeeds only in freeing the Hulk and making him bigger and stronger than before. Troops with M60 machine guns spray the 15-foot giant with bullets, but they merely annoy him like peashooter pellets. From his wrecked control centre, Ross decides it would be wiser to fight the Hulk outside.

With each transformation, the subtext of nativity is unmistakable, but more so in this instance of an induced birthing. Talbot is playing the role of a midwife from hell, and the mayhem wrought in Desert Base by the Hulk is somewhat reminiscent of the monstrous baby in Larry Cohen's cult sci-fi horror *It's Alive* (1974), in which a newborn baby slaughters the delivery room's medical staff and escapes from the hospital's maternity ward. As in *Hulk*, Cohen's satirical shocker also uses the genre metaphor of creation from Frankenstein's monster – and its title quotes directly from James Whale's version.

Father and Son

Conducting his own illicit experiments at home, David uses a hair strand to sequence Bruce's DNA to prove that Dr Krenzler is actually his own son; something he has clearly suspected for a while, despite not having seen the boy for decades. In the campus infirmary scene, David pressures Bruce to accept the truth: 'Everything your extraordinary mind has been seeking all these years, it's been inside you.' And David confesses later to passing on a genetic 'deformity' to Bruce, while nevertheless claiming it's 'an amazing strength,' too: 'And now, finally unleashed, I can harvest it.' This reveals David's hidden intentions to reclaim power from the very life that he gave to his son.

In the Desert Base scenes, Betty demands that her father help Bruce, but the distrustful and blinkered Ross is quite adamant: 'He is his father's son, every last molecule of him.' This is an inflexible viewpoint that, with all the crushingly grim inevitably of the darkest fate so often located in fairytales, coincides – albeit quite inadvertently – with David's own ad-hoc yet overambitious plans for acquiring possession of his boy's uniqueness.

While security forces raid his home, David is actually up to no good in Bruce's and Betty's Berkeley lab, where he assembles a makeshift array of gamma-ray cannons, set up for another typically reckless experiment. He inhales from a bag of nano-meds before zapping himself with radiation. Waking up from his suicidal test, David finds his blood and skin have changed in an expression of atavism, as devolutionary genotypes in his mutated DNA are activated, temporarily. But even more than that, he can meld his body with metal (like the man turning into steel in B-movie *The Most Dangerous Man Alive*). When he is interrupted by a security guard, he proudly announces: 'I can partake with the essences of all things.'

It is a moment of body horror for David, but also darkly humorous in its tone. His mutation differs radically from Bruce's changes into the Hulk because it has preserved his guileful sentience, while not stabilising his already doubtful sanity. As David merges with the room's hardware, he laughs and asks the puzzled but suspicious security guard, 'Do you really believe that I am separate from you?', and his query sounds very much like a philosophical reference to quantum theories of how the fundamental particles that compose matter simply drift through micro scales and higher energies in the fractal structure of spacetime.

In the early Marvel comics, the Absorbing Man was a super-villain created by Stan Lee and Jack Kirby in 1965. A former boxer and jailed criminal, Carl 'Crusher' Creel acquired his special powers – of absorbing the properties of anything that he touches – from the Asgardian magic of Thor's wicked brother Loki. Although David's alter-ego (credited as 'the Father' in *Hulk*) is never called the Absorbing Man, it is quite plain that the Father is based upon the character of bald brawler Creel, with unique powers that are derived from the quantum foam of material existence, but without the comicbook villain's weaponised ball-and-chain.

In the finale's hangar scene, Bruce seems resigned to his fate, until David arrives. This sequence depicts the inhuman cruelties inflicted upon a civilian locked away in a military complex (a location on Treasure Island in San Francisco Bay), where Bruce is held under threat of being tortured – apparently by electrocution – and such particularly sensationalistic images have a sinister neo-realism coming shortly after the controversial opening of a US detention camp in Guantanamo Bay. The greetings of father and son express mutual regret for

75

not killing each other when they each had a chance. Bruce is remembering his mother for the first time, but David's response is a feigned kindness, as he is completely lacking empathy. It is a dramatic scene about the impossibility of reconciliation, because David does not, in fact, want to know or even see Bruce. David thinks that his real son is the Hulk, and he comments scathingly about Bruce: 'You're nothing but a superficial shell, a husk of flimsy consciousness, ready to be torn off at a moment's notice.'

When Bruce shouts, despairingly, that he just wants his father to go away, David reacts unexpectedly: 'I'll go. You just watch me go!' He bites into a high voltage power cable and absorbs the current so he becomes an energy monster, while Bruce screams in dismay. David's manifestation is based on the Marvel super-villain called Zzzax, created by writer Steve Englehart and artist Herb Trimpe. In the comicbooks, electrical monster Zzzax was the by-product of sabotage at a nuclear power station. He became a sentient creature of pure force that first appeared, and fought the Hulk, in *The Incredible Hulk* #166 (Marvel, August 1973). It is probably just as well, though, that Zzzax is not actually mentioned in *Hulk*, as the villain's name sounds rather silly even for Marvel comics of the 1970s; despite the fascinating SF notion of a life-form composed entirely of energy.

Tapping into, or perhaps initiating, a local lightning strike, David's new form as the Father rides the discharge straight up into a cloudy sky, carrying the Hulk with him. There are strobe-lit frames like expressionist versions of comicbook splash panels for their brief sky-walk, before they fall back to earth on the edge of Pear Lake (called 'Snider Lake' in Peter David's novelisation).

The lake's irradiated waters freeze solid as a formidably violent, yet increasingly non-physical, interaction between the Hulk and the Father quickly absorbs 'all the ambient energy.' David hopes that he can finally kill the son he intended to dispose of 30 years earlier. In a surreal whirl of mental images, we journey into the deepest, darkest recesses of Bruce's troubled ego, where the teenage Bruce Krenzler and his four-year-old self watch like a captive audience to the moral dilemma.

Only the Hulk knows the solution, and the voice of his psyche yells: 'Take it all!' As in the mirror scene, the Hulk is not actually *talking* here; his line is narration, not dialogue – a prompt that momentarily blurs the distinction between diegetic and extra-diegetic sound. It is apparently a telepathic link enabled by the Father's absorbing powers. Those powers now create a vortex above the Hulk and the lake, as the Father's definitive form balloons and hovers above the water, becoming a glowing organism that looks somewhat like a gigantic swelling brain. As the Father, David has become a strange Lovecraftian abstract of cosmic potency, the living embodiment of a pulp sci-fi catastrophe, not unlike that amorphous alien creature in *The Blob* (1958, remade in 1988), but this is an *ultimate* Blob that appears capable of devouring all humanity, and perhaps the whole planet.

CHAPTER FOUR:
MYTHOLOGY UNBOUND

In the comicbook, the initial transformation of Banner into the Hulk takes place on the night of a full moon, and is followed by reversion to human form at sunrise. This early scenario by Stan Lee and Jack Kirby for the dualistic character evokes common werewolf myths. On the morning after his first change, Banner remarks: 'It feels as though a veil has been lifted – I can think again!' (*The Incredible Hulk* #1, page 11).

In the television series, after the first transformation scene (which also takes place at night) we see that the creature does not turn back into a man at dawn, so it is clear that Johnson's interpretation of the Hulk has rejected that genre element of werewolf lore. Although the movie version also sets Bruce's first change into the Hulk at the witching hour, it is not made clear if this occurs on the night of a werewolf moon.

The closing chapter of the original comicbook's origin tale sees the Hulk shot with special pellets that sap his will to resist and make him a docile slave of the villainous Gargoyle (a dwarfish mutant with an enlarged brainpan that makes him a scientific mastermind whose appearance is reviled by his Soviet comrades). This is the first time that we see the Hulk overcome by technology, and the image of an obedient Hulk following his new master is somewhat reminiscent of Rabbi Loew in command of the Golem of Prague from Jewish folklore.

The 1915 novel *The Golem* by Austrian author Gustav

Meyrink was filmed in 1920 by Paul Wegener, and his German classic silent horror is a landmark of the Weimar Republic's contribution to early cinema. This reference to the Golem in *The Incredible Hulk* #1 is also the first instance of a recurring motif of power – brawn versus brains – that formed the crux of several other comicbook adventures to come. Bruce's and the Hulk's encounters with Talbot in *Hulk* may be viewed as a further – albeit minor key – recycling of the Golem motif, as Talbot's eager attempts to harness the Hulk's power are a codified form of enslavement.

In the pilot movie for the TV series, Banner is stalked and frequently troubled by a nosey reporter named Jack McGee (Jack Colvin). McGee works for a newspaper called the *National Register* (a *National Inquirer* style tabloid). He is investigating reported sightings of a giant creature and thinks, at first, that he is chasing clues to a Bigfoot story. The legendary Bigfoot, alias Sasquatch (and sometimes dubbed America's Abominable Snowman), was all the rage during the 1970s, following widely published photos from a sequence of 16mm cine footage shot in 1967.

While the fringe sciences of cryptozoological studies were frequently troubled by hoaxes, Bigfoot provided an ideal reference point for *The Incredible Hulk* on TV. It would make any appearances of the creature within the fictional narratives of serial drama easy to dismiss as practical jokes and, with real world scepticism increased by scientific debunking of Bigfoot reports, any evidence would become immediately suspect, if not obviously fraudulent. Linking the Hulk to Bigfoot stories was a shrewd move by Johnson (who had previously used Bigfoot as a character in episodes of *The Six Million Dollar Man*), and enabled the delicate balancing act of veracity in a fantastical sci-fi adventure to be maintained.

Ang Lee's *Hulk* pays tribute to both the comicbook's creator and the TV series' star in an early cameo scene for Stan Lee and Lou Ferrigno as a pair of campus guards. Lee is chatting amiably throughout the photo-op and has a droll one-liner in-joke, 'Security ought to be beefed up', spoken while the former Mr Universe and television's Hulk walks along beside him.

Because the movie combines the pulp mythology of the comicbook with elements from the strikingly different television version, *Hulk* is an artistic adaptation that is far more like the final movement of a musical suite than simply another spin-off in a standard media franchise.

Instead of prominent references to the varied folklore of Wolfman, Golem and Bigfoot, as seen in both comicbook and television series, the movie adopts a very different set of mythic analogies, each one linked to sequences where Bruce becomes the Hulk.

Atlas

During the movie's first transformation sequence, when the Hulk smashes through walls in Bruce's and Betty's laboratory, he reaches the larger space where the gamma-sphere is housed. He pulls the machine loose from its base, and then crouches to hoist it up and balance it on his shoulders. This is the Hulk in his Atlas pose, a blatantly symbolic imitation of the titan from

Greek myths. Atlas is a figure often depicted in sculptures as supporting the weight of the world on his shoulders, so it is a particularly apt allusion to Bruce's quite overwhelming angst. This is the first and most obvious example of references to mythical strongmen in *Hulk*.

Solidly-built hardware, the gamma-sphere is reportedly about seven feet in diameter, and weighs about 14 tons. The prop was actually a gamma detector/microscope, on loan from the Argonne National Laboratory near Chicago. Historically, the ANL site is associated with the Manhattan Project to create the first atomic bomb. When the Hulk hurls the machine straight through an outer wall, it falls onto a police car, crushing the vehicle, and splits into a pair of hemispheres. The wobbling halves of the wrecked gamma-sphere (one of the most difficult CGI renderings ever created by ILM, according to Ang Lee's DVD commentary track) represent Bruce's shattered world, and perhaps the planet Earth – which the power of the Hulk may eventually break asunder.

Hercules

In addition to the obvious *Cujo* homage, and the subtle twist of tripling *The Hound of the Baskervilles*, the Hulk's battle against a pack of three dogs has a mythological analogy in the Greco-Roman story of the demigod Hercules versus Cerberus. In the ancient myths, Cerberus was a three-headed dog guarding a gateway to the underworld. The defeat of Cerberus by Hercules was the last of his epical 12 labours of atonement. Some versions of the Hercules myth state that he captured but did not actually kill Cerberus, but other tough jobs on the hero's to-do list included killing a mighty lion with his bare hands, trapping a monstrous boar, and then capturing the Cretan bull (a source of the minotaur legend). So, however we may choose to interpret any of these mythical riffs in *Hulk*, the battles of Hercules against chimeric animals have an intriguing relevance to the Hulk's extraordinarily vicious fighting and killing of three mutant dogs. The sequence depicts its comicbook styled action and B-movie horrors with a quite extraordinary brutality, and is the first veritably feral *hulkgasm* of Ang Lee's movie.

Samson

In the cabin, after the Hulk's battle against the mutant dogs, Betty is sure that she has done the right thing, arguably the best thing for all concerned, by contacting her father to ask for help, without informing Bruce. Although the Hulk saved Betty from the dogs, she is simply too scared to face the enormity that the Hulk problem represents for Bruce. It is, though, a fully rational decision for Betty to betray Bruce to her father. Betty is wise enough to realise that she cannot help Bruce, effectively, without Ross's military assistance.

Betty's betrayal of Bruce, in order to rob him of his Hulk strength, recalls Samson and Delilah – a Hebrew version of superhuman strongman myths. Samson fought a lion (symbolised by the Hulk's struggles against Talbot), killed an army of philistines (here, US military forces, led by Ross) and later demolished a pagan temple (represented by the havoc that the Hulk causes in the Desert Base).

However, in the myth of Samson, Delilah schemes to discover the secret of Samson's power and learns that cutting his hair removes his strength. In *Hulk*, it is David who takes Bruce's hair (sequenced for DNA to confirm that Bruce is his son), but Betty soon learns the secret of Bruce's identity when she visits David. This thread of narrative in *Hulk* sketches the biblical story of Samson in purely allegorical form, so that we can add Samson to the four mythological figures given symbolic treatment here.

Goliath

After the vandalism at the Berkeley labs that results from Bruce's first transformation, the Hulk pauses and steps forward out of the shadows to see his first human. David peeks – almost meekly, but in awe – from the janitor's storage room. The CGI character of the Hulk is ready for his first big close-up. His performance opposite Nolte's father figure is just as compelling as the real actor's expression of mixed wonder and terror. As David reaches up, the Hulk looks down with curiosity. The comparatively small man's hand strokes the Hulk's jaw and cheek, tenderly, as David recalls playing monster-fighting games with his young son. But, for the Hulk, this encounter with and recognition of David triggers a return of the painful memory of what happened to Bruce's mother (a memory blocked to Bruce himself). The recollection sparks a flight – not a fight – response, which drives the Hulk to escape through the roof into the night sky above the city by the bay. David cowers on the floor, trembling and crying: 'My Bruce.' David has met his true son for the first time. This is an analogy to the moment of David first meeting Goliath in the Old Testament biblical myth. It also foreshadows the ultimate confrontation between father and son in the movie's closing sequence.

The last chapter of the *Hulk* story is a stunning visualisation of the abstract, shifting from a dramatisation of metabolic changes in meta-human beings to a quite startling revelation of the metaphysical realm. The Hulk versus the Father is a final reprise of that earlier allegory of the David and Goliath meeting in the ruined Berkeley lab. The death of giant Goliath is the fourth allegorical depiction of a mythic strongman in *Hulk*, but it is presented with a distinctive twist. In the familiar Old Testament story, David slew Goliath with a single stone launched from a slingshot. In this movie's witty parody, David *becomes* the stone, when the Father turns into a rocky creature. The Hulk wrestles with this stone man but, when the Father starts absorbing his power and strength, and momentarily subdues him, he does not manage to kill his opponent. Although David is eventually the loser in their titanic struggle, it is only when their figurative roles are reserved (as when the Hulk/Bruce becomes *David* of the TV series), and the Father becomes the overbearing aggressor – in a psychic assault upon his own son's innocent will – that any resolution to the final conflict becomes possible.

We see Bruce *Krenzler* (now, no longer identifiable as the defeated Banner's son), floating alone, underwater, and apparently unharmed, as if the cosmic energy's dissipation took all of the Hulk's strength to survive, leaving only Bruce alive. At last, he is free of his father's malign influence. Bruce is less than a monster but more than a man.

Man Versus Machines

The comicbook sees the Hulk disarm a Russian spy, and he crushes the man's revolver in one mighty hand. It is a crucial scene in constructing the Hulk's mythology, because it demonstrates the creature's attitude to weaponry and presents the irony that, while Banner built a super-bomb for the military, the Hulk proactively opposes any/all devices of warfare, which obviously includes the invention that created him. This is a kind of moral stance on militarism that is reflected in the lengthy rampage scenes of *Hulk*. It is a timely reminder that, in the 21st Century, pacifism is not passive. The Hulk is not trying to win a war against the machines, but he fully intends to end it. Furthermore, in *Hulk*, the newly-born creature of science destroys the gamma-sphere that has created him, presenting a position of abhorrence towards technology, whether it is relatively benign or not.

From a close-up shot of Bruce unconscious, sealed in a coffin-like metal cylinder, we zoom out to a busy montage of helicopters flying over the desert. The cargo container holding Bruce captive is carried beneath a Sikorsky S-64 Skycrane. There is a Bell AH-1 Cobra gunship escort, bristling with missile racks and rocket pods, and a Bell 212 Twin Huey transport. These are genuine rotorcraft, not CGI, and they add widescreen spectacle to this exhilarating airborne sequence (in fact, nothing adds impressive production values to action movies better than helicopters!), which benefits from the energy of a drumbeat score, and the further use of attention grabbing split-screens again evoking comicbook panels. The helicopters rendezvous with a convoy of armoured vehicles that enter Desert Base via a hangar symbolically marked *Victory*, with the US flag painted on its big sliding doors. It is the gateway to a vast underground complex, where Bruce's security pod (dubbed 'beer-can' by the movie's crew) slides down a 45-degree angled access shaft.

This dialogue-free sequence establishes that Bruce is a helpless victim of technology. It is a situation that can be remedied only by the third appearance of the Hulk, who escapes from the maximum security containment facility of Desert Base with only a little difficulty. The Hulk bursts into daylight, symbolically smashing through the victory flag on the hangar doors, and he accelerates into a 300-mph run, before jumping into the ruined town. This begins the movie's centrepiece, a series of linked action sequences illustrating an Odyssean journey homeward, and the popular genre theme of man (in this analogy, the singularly-mutated Hulk, of course) against war machines.

The Hulk's brief abstraction in the ruined town is disturbed by the first bombing raid, starting with a fuel-air-explosive (FAE) thermo-baric weapon dropping on a house. Leaping above the cluster bombs, the Hulk becomes a tiny figure, which grants a fresh sense of scale to widescreen landscape shots. The Hulk does not run away from the four M1 Abrams battle tanks; he jumps and then runs towards his attackers, charging like a bull, and bellowing his defiance just as he did with the mutant dogs. The Hulk wields a broken tank turret just like it is a caveman's club. However, instead of using it to wreck his foe's machine, the Hulk simply bends the turret of the last tank so it points back into the crew cabin's hatch. It is a familiar feat of strength from *The Incredible Hulk* comicbook, and even today it is one of the most potent images of enforced disarmament ever devised.

'Angry Man is un-secure,' Ross reports, directly to the US President – who is fishing in the movie, but golfing in the novelisation (where author Peter David notes sarcastically: 'American tax dollars at work'). Leaving the wreckage of tanks in his dust, the Hulk is on the run again, jumping even higher to cover miles of desert in brief airborne moments. There is an ecstatic sense of freedom in his speeding through such glorious travelogue scenery of the rugged American southwest. Set to Arabian style music, these images of movement over beautiful landscapes form a counterpoint to the CGI stunts in Sam Raimi's *Spider-Man* trilogy (2002-2007), where the young hero swings upon his web-lines between towering buildings across the city. That is how Spidey gets around town, but *Hulk* establishes an entirely new spacious aesthetic of motion. There is a wonderful sense of exhilaration to the Hulk's progress in mighty bounds that is simply far more fascinating to watch than even Superman's flying abilities – which are, arguably, best depicted in Bryan Singer's tribute movie *Superman Returns* (2006).

Ross orders the pilots of Comanche helicopters into combat with guns and Hellfire missiles, but the Hulk is fast enough to dodge most of their attacks. The Hulk snatches one missile in mid air, bites off the warhead and spits it directly at a low-flying helicopter, which crashes onto the valley floor. The remaining Comanches of Tango flight pursue the Hulk into a massive sandstone formation, and Ross orders: 'Salvo all. Turn it into a parking lot.' The bombardment levels a wide area, burying the Hulk under countless tons of shattered rock. 'T-bolt, your parking lot is ready,' quips the departing pilot.

Although the RAH-66 Comanche stealth helicopter was in fact a real machine, developed for the US military by Boeing-Sikorsky, that weapons research programme was cancelled in February 2004, after spending $40 billion over 20 years, without a production version, and with only two prototypes built. In *Hulk*, the Comanche helicopters are entirely virtual work, as the production's aerial co-ordinator Craig Hosking explains:

'The Comanche was all digital. We used, what is becoming a common practice of flying, a target aircraft. Several scenes were filmed by ground cameras as well as the Space-cam on another helicopter. I flew a Eurocopter AS 350-B2 which had reference marks painted on it. The cameras filmed me performing the manoeuvres that the Comanche was called upon to fly. The reference marks on the A-Star are then tracked by the computer and transferred to the digital model,

allowing the computer guys to make it look much more realistic when it flies. It particularly helps them achieve the proper bank-angle versus rate-of-turn look. I have used this technique on many occasions.'
(Rotary Action website, www.rotaryaction.com)

Having survived premature burial, the Hulk leaps into San Francisco bay, landing atop the Golden Gate Bridge, where Ross calls up an air strike by a pair of USAF jets. One plane rolls out of control, heading for the bridge, but the Hulk saves the day, heroically, by jumping onto the fighter so his weight drops its altitude and it safely flies under the bridge. Ross orders the pilot: 'Take him on a ride to the top of the world. Let's see what the thin air will do for him.' Clinging to the aircraft at its maximum altitude, the Hulk travels to the edge of space, but falls back down to earth. The scene is a reference to Philip Kaufman's *The Right Stuff* (1983), in which test-pilot Chuck Yeager (Sam Shepard) flies an experimental plane. Despite the use of CG animation for the F-22 Raptors (which did not enter active USAF service until 2007), this aerial sequence has far superior visual effects to earlier action movies with hi-tech aircraft, such as Clint Eastwood's *Firefox* (1982). Watching from the JTFW base (a set on the manmade Treasure Island, formerly the site of an actual US Navy base), Betty sees the Hulk splash down in the bay, and she explains to her father why it is a very bad idea for the military to try to destroy him: 'You'll only fuel his rage, and you'll make him stronger.'

In the Marvel milieu, the anti-heroic Hulk is very much a force of nature – like any tornado, hurricane or earthquake – so mankind and all manmade constructions will usually be the losers in direct conflicts with him. It is a hard lesson that Ross learns here, at the cost of his elite forces and the most sophisticated weaponry at his command.

Symbolic Medley

Between the original comicbook and its adaptation for the popular genre TV series, the green monster of unbound rage became a sub-cultural idol. But even before Stan Lee and Jack Kirby created *The Incredible Hulk*, the notion of a jolly green giant had a symbolic existence. In Minnesota, USA, a famous cannery of vegetables has used a Green Giant as its official logo since 1928. A 50-foot statue of this company mascot was erected in the river valley, a year after *The Incredible Hulk* premiered on TV, and so the Green Giant became a successful advertising icon. I remember adverts for Green Giant products, placed – quite amusingly – in commercial breaks during episodes of the Hulk TV series.

A popular character from comic-strips and cartoons since the 1930s, Popeye the sailor was portrayed by Robin Williams in Robert Altman's cult live-action movie adaptation in 1980. Although considered by many to be the first superhero strongman, Popeye cannot escape the suspicion that he was created at least partly to help sell spinach, and this tenuous link to prodigious strength derived from a green source makes him one of the most overlooked forebears of the Hulk, if only in retrospect.

The Hulk is produced by a kind of Immaculate Conception, as he is an innocent who is free from sin; or perhaps just an accidental rebirth prompted by the unchecked curiosity of a maverick scientist. Both the mythic and scientific interpretations are fitting, and add another layer of duality to the character. *Hulk* is a standalone movie, yet it is still a part of the continuing legacy of a giant-sized superhero without a costume.

Although the Hulk should not be mistaken for philosopher Friedrich Nietzsche's notion of the übermensch (or 'over-man'), he is quite obviously a stubborn and irascible nonconformist, who has rejected many of conventional society's norms. Superheroes should not be viewed as just icons of fascism. They are larger-than-life, inspirational figures for a more humanitarian future. Even when viewed as an imperfect creation (which he is), the Hulk is a mutation that represents the possibilities for genetic-engineering of humans after the advancement of current science. Talbot's moneymaking plan for indestructible super-soldiers is a blinkered notion. Bruce understands the potential better, and recognises that nano-medical research could physically and mentally improve the lives of all humans.

If ultimate freedom is the primal realm of the gods, then the Hulk is a top contender. But it is possible (and favourable!) to fight the good fight without any need for a crutch of faith – because scientific uncertainty is, quite paradoxically, our greatest source of strength. In the vastly complex multiverse of superhero movies, Ang Lee's *Hulk*, like Stan Lee's comicbook creation, is the strongest one there is.

Much like the protagonist tagged Number Six in Patrick McGoohan's classic TV series *The Prisoner* (1967), the definitive version of the Hulk in Ang Lee's *Hulk* claims 'the right to be an individual' – no matter what the circumstances. And yet the Hulk also has to play the brutish role of a 21st Century poster boy for asserting hyper-masculine concerns in our post-feminist era. Despite Ang Lee's keenly innovative and highbrow approach to *Hulk*, any heroic or antiheroic being must become the embodiment of action. Doing all of this successfully is not easy when you are green.

In Sidney Lumet's satirical drama *Network* (1976), news anchorman Howard Beale (Peter Finch) rants on live TV, 'I'm mad as hell and I'm not gonna take this anymore!', and his catchphrase becomes a rallying call for a social rebellion. Like angry sage Beale, criticising the hypocrisy of an exploitative corporate system, the Hulk represents the incoherent protests of the so-called 99 percent. In our bleakest era of authoritarian indifference to human suffering, the duality of the anti-heroic character of the Hulk is able to expose the dystopian/apocalyptic dangers, both ethical and moral, that are posed by the unchecked growth of capitalism.

Gestalt Mythos

If the 21st Century's alchemical marriage of global corporate politics and religious extremism lurches away from the rationalist mindset of secular humanism – towards a new dark age of Orwellian censorship, oppressive laws, and profitable wars – such a back-step can be countered only by new philosophical judgements where global knowledge trumps local ignorance. *Hulk* represents a grand myth for our time. We all have a monster of rage like the Hulk inside us and – like Bruce Krenzler becoming Bruce Banner – we must learn to embrace our inherited faults and tame them with a New Enlightenment, before that rough beast of green ire controls us. The great effectiveness of the Hulk as an agent of change (in a world beset by our paranoid tendencies and thoughtlessly self-destructive impulses) reminds us that although we live in an era when one insane person might destroy the world, it is also possible (yet increasingly unlikely, admittedly) that one wise individual could save it.

B-movie motifs recur throughout *Hulk*, like the allegorical scenes of cathartic (killing the mutant dogs) or corrosive (fighting the Hulk's father) violence. Packed with themes of psychological horror, borrowings from the science fiction and fantasy genres, many wry and witty tributes to specific works, *Hulk* transcends its miscellaneous allusions, influences, metaphors, subgenre emblems, scenes of homage, and vast complexity of subversive symbolism erupting from depictions of rapidly expanding narrative scales (from indoors, to the great outdoors, over continental ranges to suborbital ascension, and a submersive dive into seemingly infinite inner-space), so the movie's array of images are all woven together perfectly in an organic fashion. In short, Ang Lee's *Hulk* is much more than the sum of its parts.

The poignant double-coda, of Betty's phone call from her apologetic dad, and the fugitive Bruce warning in Spanish 'You're making me angry. You wouldn't like me when I'm angry' (again quoting from the TV series) to the bullying militiamen who are stealing medical supplies in the South American jungle, sets up numerous possibilities for a sequel to *Hulk* but, unfortunately, that was not to be. The screen fades out to green, the end credits scroll, and Danny Elfman's haunting theme music is shunted aside in favour of a rather typical US rock anthem, 'Set Me Free' by super-group wannabes Velvet Revolver. The song was included on *Hulk*'s soundtrack release, and on the band's own debut album, *Contraband* (RCA, 2004).

APPENDIX: GAMMA GUIDE: CLASSIC & REBOOT

Calm down, it's only a movie …

Hulk received mixed reviews, earning a 5.7 rating on Internet Movie Database (www.imdb.com), a grade B and 62/100 review metric on the Movie Review Query Engine (www.mrqe.com), and a 62 percent score on the Rotten Tomatoes site (www.rottentomatoes.com). Clearly, *Hulk* is the most misunderstood and often unfairly criticised superhero/ monster movie of recent years. However, from the critical mass of misinterpretations and many other thoughtless tabloid-style reactions to Ang Lee's masterpiece, two insightful reviews stand out:

'*Hulk* brings to the fore the pervasively non-naturalistic, fairytale quality of [Ang] Lee's work … The film also foregrounds the fable-like element of oedipal conflict … In Lee's films nuclear families are combustible and destructive, like those bombs that are numbly witnessed in *Hulk*. There's a mythical wickedness at large … This is CGI in the service of surrealism … The various visual devices make up a rattle-bag aesthetic … but it's in another league of complexity and for this reason is the best Marvel adaptation so far.'

Rob White, 'The Main Attraction' (featured review), pages 34-35, *Sight & Sound* – Volume 13 #8, August 2003

'All the Marvel films have been careful to try and respect their originals' resonance as hormonal parables addressing the issues that beset the comics fan at the pubertal cusp of his purchasing commitment: alienation, self-esteem, identity, body change, sexual un-success, and in *Hulk*'s case savage mood swings … [Ang] Lee's clearly thought about ways in which the narrative density of the film image can be enhanced for an ever more impatient and sophisticated consumer'

Nick Lowe, 'Mutant Popcorn' (regular column), page 45,
Interzone #191, September 2003

Browsing some of the negative comments about *Hulk* that can be found online, it appears that Ang Lee's movie divided the opinions of both critics and fans. My theory is that many followers of the Hulk character in Marvel comicbooks were rather disappointed that, although the Hulk is in fact an excellent CGI character with a full set of super-powers, he does not talk at all in this movie. On the other hand, viewers who still had fond memories of the TV series, where the Hulk did not speak, may have been dissatisfied with this animated rendering of the character they best remember as being played by a bodybuilder in green greasepaint.

Hulk Rule of Fours – A Recap:

- Genre influences: *Frankenstein*, Jekyll and Hyde, *King Kong, Beauty and the Beast*.
- Principal characters: Bruce, Betty, David, Ross.

- Animal DNA samples: jellyfish, sea cucumber, starfish, lizard.
- Prime causes: nano-meds, gamma-rays, mutant DNA, emotional damage.
- Hulk-out triggers: anxiety, fear, anger, despair.
- Four transformations into the Hulk, each more powerful than the last.
- Bruce awakens from his recurring nightmare on four occasions.
- Mythological strongman allegories: Atlas, Hercules, Samson, Goliath.
- Colour scheme (blue, red, yellow, green) used for Desert Base's main hall set.
- Four Abrams battle tanks (score: Hulk 4 … tanks 0).
- Four Comanche attack helicopters (score: Hulk 2 … helicopters 0).
- A gamma-bomb mushroom cloud appears four times in *Hulk*.
- Four dosages of nano-meds are used in experiments on-screen: for Freddie the frog, Bruce, a lab rat, David.
- ACGT (coincidentally!) – nucleic acids in DNA: adenine, thymine, cytosine, guanine.
- The movie's title was reduced from *The Incredible Hulk*, to *The Hulk*, to four-letter *Hulk*.

We could also add: Bruce was orphaned as a four-year-old, and Betty's dad is a four-star general.

Five Years Later ...

Three decades after *The Incredible Hulk* TV series, French-born director Louis Leterrier made a nominal sequel and movie franchise reboot, *The Incredible Hulk* (2008), for Marvel. Unhappily, it is a re-cast production with a different approach to its comicbook material, which results in a spineless, ad-hoc and clichéd plot about reunited lovers (Bruce and Betty), all hinging upon the Hulk's violent confrontations with psychotic revenger Emil Blonsky (Tim Roth).

Whereas *Hulk* paid reverential tributes to its diverse inspirations and genre movie sources, *The Incredible Hulk* simply and obviously steals, and engages in blatant style theft. Its piracy is almost random, beginning with an ill-conceived montage that fails to remix the varied origin stories of the Hulk from the TV series and Ang Lee's *Hulk*, while adding some retcon changes from recent Hulk comicbooks. The cascade of imagery is flippant. Edward Norton's Bruce winks at Liv Tyler's Betty; but he is also winking blatantly at viewers, as if to say, 'Hey, guys, I'm starring in a comicbook movie. Yay for me!' The intro is also cluttered. There are SHIELD and Stark references, and hints about super-soldier experiments. It is a medley of geeky in-jokes, with none of the carefully compiled revisionism that distinguished *Hulk* from its erstwhile Marvel movie stablemates.

It is especially disappointing in that, in sharp contrast to the accidental creation of the Hulk (a scientific mishap) presented in Stan Lee's original comicbook and repeated in Ang Lee's *Hulk*, Leterrier's version reinterprets the character's origin as a partly intentional by-product of super-soldier research (only a Pyrrhic victory for science) with a vague continuity from the *Captain America* comicbook series.

Driven by its conspiracy-theory shenanigans and spy-movie action set-pieces, Leterrier's movie tackles the retconned Hulk of 2004's *The Ultimates* comicbook series created by Mark Millar and Bryan Hitch. This 'Ultimate Avengers' reworking of the Hulk's origin is presented with a far better science fictional veracity in the Warren Ellis and Cary Nord graphic novel *Ultimate Human* (Marvel, 2008), an excellent four-issue series that revised the Hulk origin via SF extrapolation.

Ang Lee's *Hulk* showcased the beauty of nature. Leterrier's movie begins with shots of a Brazilian location, showcasing a colourful hillside *favela* – which looks pretty at first glance until we realise it is just a vast, sprawling slum. In the bottling plant shootout ('Something big hit *us!*'), the factory resembles scenes from *The Terminator* (1984), *Terminator 2: Judgement Day* (1991) and the industrial noir settings of *Aliens* (1986). We see Betty and the Hulk in a cave near a waterfall, and this scene is copied, shamelessly, from Peter Jackson's *King Kong* (2005) remake.

In the Mexican scenes, where Bruce is reduced to the status of a street beggar, Joseph Harnell's 'The Lonely Man' theme from *The Incredible Hulk* TV series is recycled, quite cynically, and there is no respect at all for the dignified composition. Here, Bruce is reliant more upon his wits than his scientific intelligence, but vacuous actor Norton seems more interested in ensuring that his role is slickly heroic – like Hollywood's template for male leads – and he does not portray Bruce as a very smart man, anyway: 'Don't make me hungry. You wouldn't like me when I'm hungry.'

Simplistic expository dialogue inhibits narrative pacing and weakens the quality of cinematic storytelling. Sappy romantic scenes are mostly just Hollywood clichés, and there is even a contrived kissing-in-the-rain moment. The principal characters are presented as mere stereotypes: Bruce (haunted yet brave drifter), Betty (shallow ex-girlfriend), Ross (gruff old soldier), Blonsky (homicidal maniac). The sci-fi content is a slapdash mix of hi-tech sonic weapons and some present-day hardware (like the CGI for a Boeing AH-64 Apache helicopter). One urban action sequence, shot in a first-person-shooter mode, is so superficially trendy in its pre-millennial videogame imagery that it looks dated and is painfully cringeworthy to watch.

The Hulk's opponent here, a super-villain called the Abomination (Blonsky, after his makeover), is a hideous creature who talks too much to be taken very seriously as a monster-character. The Hulk versus the Abomination street-fight has its bullet-time action obviously copied from *The Matrix* trilogy (1999-2003). A signature line from the original comicbooks, 'Hulk smash!', never makes any sense at all from a psychological standpoint. Seriously, why does the Hulk talk about himself in the third person here? It works in the comicbooks, but not in movies or on TV. Any creature of unbridled rage would act on instinct, without self-awareness (but probably would not like it if people called him names).

Leterrier's movie has a CGI Hulk that looks dirty and ugly, and is rather more grotesque than is necessary. Such a demeanour makes him a far less sympathetic character, even though the Hulk is more man-shaped here, unlike the proverbial mountain of muscle in Ang Lee's superior *Hulk*. I do actually like Leterrier's *The Incredible Hulk*, because it is good fun at times, but it is a re-imagining that is no match for Ang Lee's more poetic and cerebral take on the character, so it fails to equal the artistic triumphs of *Hulk*.

Leterrier's disposable *The Incredible Hulk* is ineffective as a remake, profoundly flawed as a sequel and a cheesy comicbook effort with a throwback attitude, not a modern cinematic adaptation of a popular mythos. Its main purpose is to retcon the big-screen Hulk characterisation into a franchise-friendly version – a manageable jigsaw piece to fit into the crossover epic narrative of Joss Whedon's *Avengers Assemble*. In the end, I was left thinking (just like Blonsky asks of the Hulk): 'Is that all you've got?'

Teamwork

As he is an anarchistic loner, can the Hulk ever fit in? Joss Whedon's event movie *Avengers Assemble* (2012) combines the characters of four Marvel movies (including Jon Favreau's *Iron Man 2*, Kenneth Branagh's *Thor*, and Joe Johnston's *Captain America: The First Avenger*), and blends together an original *Avengers* canon plot with post-*Hulk* retcon comicbook series *The Ultimates*. With a re-cast Bruce (Mark Ruffalo, who played a detective alongside Robert Downey Jr in David Fincher's true-crime drama *Zodiac*, 2007), *Avengers Assemble* fields a different style and tone in its approach to comicbook superheroes. Whereas Ang Lee's *Hulk* grants plenty of solo screen-time to the man and the monster, Whedon's movie maintains a pace that avoids introspection and concentrates upon lively ensemble performances, so Bruce (and the Hulk, too) must interact closely with the other superheroes, instead of the Hulk being the first digital movie star in a performance measured against great actors.

The Hulk in *Avengers Assemble* is less a monster and more like just another fighting agent alongside the costumed heroes. The Hulk is simply the big gun (or 'a time-bomb') of the super-team. Nevertheless, *Avengers Assemble* is constructed with such enthusiasm and efficiency that Whedon manages to channel the Hulk's rage into set-pieces that score highly as reworked clichés of urban disaster movies (plus alien invasion adventures). The Hulk is cleverly installed into a sci-fi/fantasy narrative, accomplishing the nifty trick of introducing a team of heroes fighting – not only together, but as one.

HULK

138 minutes (12 / PG-13) 2003
Widescreen aspect ratio 1.85:1
Universal Pictures

Main cast:
Eric Bana … Bruce Krenzler / Banner
Jennifer Connelly … Betty Ross
Sam Elliott … General Thaddeus 'Thunderbolt' Ross
Josh Lucas … Glenn Talbot
Nick Nolte … David Banner / Father
Paul Kersey … young David Banner
Cara Buono … Edith Banner
Todd Tesen … young Captain Ross
Kevin Rankin … Jake Harper
Celia Weston … Mrs Monica Krenzler
Mike Erwin … teenage Bruce Krenzler
Lou Ferrigno … security guard
Stan Lee … security guard

Producers: Gale Anne Hurd, Avi Arad, James Schamus, and Larry Franco
Story by James Schamus
Screenplay by John Turman, Michael France, and James Schamus
Based upon the Marvel comic book character created by Stan Lee and Jack Kirby

Production design by Rick Heinrichs

Costume design by Marit Allen

Cinematography by Frederick Elmes

Editing by Tim Squyres

Music by Danny Elfman

Special visual effects by ILM

Directed by Ang Lee

Cinema releases – UK: 18 July 2003; USA: 20 June 2003

DVD & VHS – UK: 17 November 2003; USA: 28 October 2003

HD-DVD – 12 December 2006

Blu-ray – UK: 17 November 2008; USA: 16 September 2008

Novelisation: *Hulk* by Peter David, Boxtree paperback, 16 May 2003

Original soundtrack album (Danny Elfman, et al), Decca, 21 July 2003

ABOUT THE AUTHOR

Tony Lee edits SF/horror fiction and genre poetry for *Premonitions* magazine-anthology (see PigasusPress.co.uk), maintains *VideoVista*.net and Zone-SF.com non-fiction websites, and created the unique *RotaryAction*.com. His regular columns of DVD and Blu-ray reviews appear in *Interzone* (covering SF/fantasy) and *Black Static* (horror/fantasy), both published by TTA Press.